MONEY MANAGEMENT WORKSHEETS

FOR

1-2-3/™ SYMPHONY™

NICK MAFFEI

TAB BOOKS Inc.

Blue Ridge Summit, PA 17214

This book is dedicated
to my wife Betty,
whose patience and understanding
made it possible,

and

to my son David,
who inspired me

FIRST EDITION

FIRST PRINTING

Copyright © 1985 by TAB BOOKS Inc.
Printed in the United States of America

Library of Congress Cataloging in Publication Data

Maffei, Nick.
Money management worksheets for 1-2-3™/Symphony™

Includes index.
1. Finance, Personal—Data processing. 2. LOTUS
1-2-3 (Computer program) 3. Symphony (Computer
program). I. Title. II. Title: Money management
worksheets for one-two-three™ /Symphony™
HG179.M5965 1985   332.024′0028′542 ^ 84-26899
ISBN 0-8306-0968-7
ISBN 0-8306-1968-2 (pbk.)

Contents

Introduction

Everyone has a dream. Mine has always been to make my fortune quickly, retire early, and live off my investments. Until recently, however, all my attempts to do so have met with little success. But once I gave up the notion of instant wealth and discovered the power of the personal computer as an investment tool, my fortunes began to improve.

At first I imagined that all I had to do was set up my finances on my PC, sit back and watch my assets appreciate. Well, it didn't work out that way, but along the way I learned a few things.

The first thing I had to do was learn about money and computers. While many books have been written about personal money management, few provide you with the means to accomplish it on a home computer. And even though I have an MBA degree in finance and several years of experience in data processing, I had to teach myself how to use my personal computer to manage my investments. It was slow work, with lots of trial and error. I became sophisticated only through long hours of practice.

When I first planned this book, I thought it would include examples of successful money management worksheets as developed by the experts in the field. But as I studied these worksheets and compared them to my own, I found that while theirs were sometimes interesting, they were seldom personal enough for me to use. Each person's goals and lifestyle are different. What is appropriate for one is not practical for another.

That's why this is a do-it-yourself book. It shows you step by step how to use Lotus 1-2-3 or Symphony to construct dozens of simple but practical financial worksheets and provides a full explanation of how to use these worksheets to create your own personalized financial statements.

More than 60 sample worksheets are presented, and they cover a variety of money management applications, ranging from personal financial statements and investment analyses to budget forecasts and retirement planning. These models are an outgrowth of several years experience in working with and teaching personal computer applications. The variety of models and ideas is guaranteed to stimulate your thoughts about your own personal finances and suggest a wide range of potential applications.

If you enjoy managing your own investments, enjoy doing things for yourself, and enjoy the personal computer, then you will find this book useful. By following the step-by-step approach spelled out in the chapters of this book, you will begin to reap the profits and rewards of managing your personal finances yourself.

SECTION 1
WHAT THIS
BOOK WILL DO FOR YOU

This Book's Purpose

This book introduces you to a new way to use your computer and manage your money. It shows you how your home computer can help to organize your personal finances and save you time and money.

MONEY AND COMPUTERS

If you have never used a computer before, this book will save you hours of trial and error. If you are already a sophisticated user, this book will stimulate your thinking and provide you with a host of new ideas and techniques.

More than 60 practical and ready-to-use financial worksheets are presented in a logical fashion from the simple to the complex. You don't need to be a financial or computer expert to use or interpret the reports in this book. All you need is a little common sense and the ability to follow easy, nontechnical step-by-step instructions. Most of the worksheets are one-page reports and are easy to understand and simple to construct. If you can add and subtract, you can understand and build these worksheets.

This book dispels much of the mystery of money management and shows you how to get started on your own personal financial plan using the Lotus 1-2-3 or Symphony programs. It offers hundreds of ideas for putting your plan into action. Some may apply to your personal situation, others may not. In either case the variety of worksheets will suggest a wide range of potential applications which will make it easy for you to account for your past financial activity, your current net worth and your future cash flow.

DON'T GET RID OF YOUR TAX ADVISOR

The intent of this book is not to make you into a financial expert, nor is it intended to replace the advice and services of your accountant or professional financial planner. Since each investor's situation is unique, I recommend that you continue with your present advisor and that you always consult a professional before making any complex financial decision.

Furthermore, this book does not offer specific investment or estate planning advice. It does, however, provide you with basic concepts and practices that apply universally to sound financial management. It will help you spot potential financial problems and show you how to avoid them. It will guide you through the maze of accounting and technical terms so that you can concentrate on your personal finances.

Even with all the help and assistance in this book, there is no denying that successful money management requires time and discipline. But it can be achieved by anyone who sets goals and sticks to them.

How To Use This Book

The design of the book makes it easy for readers, even those who have never used a computer before, to find their own level of expertise. Many of the worksheets presented in this book can be used directly to meet individual needs, or they easily can be modified to meet specific requirements. If you desire, you can do a complete overhaul of your personal finances. If you need help only in specific areas, you can concentrate on those parts of the book.

THIS BOOK IS DESIGNED TO HELP YOU

The book is divided into seven major sections which makes it easy for you to go directly to your area of special interest without having to read through information that may already be familiar. As you complete each chapter, you will understand what financial information is required to create the various worksheets in that section. The seven sections are as follows:

Section 1, "What This Book Will Do For You," explains the basic format of the book and how to use it.

Section 2, "Money and the Personal Computer," provides information about the required computer hardware and software used in the sample worksheets and discusses the advantages of using a personal computer to manage your money.

Section 3, "Getting Started," is one of the most important sections in the book. It offers suggestions on how to begin your financial management program and how to customize your worksheets. It also assists you in defining your goals and provides a dramatic example of how to become a millionaire.

Section 4, "Family and Financial Records," looks at specific aspects of personal finance such as a personal financial statement, budgets, and cash flow. It also provides examples of forms for recording vital personal information.

Section 5, "Planning," provides you with examples and illustrations of how to manage your assets in specific areas like taxes, insurance, education and retirement.

Section 6, "Investments," explores some of the more sophisticated areas of personal finance such

as portfolio management, investment planning, and the analysis of real estate.

Section 7, "Getting Good Results," offers criteria to help you monitor and evaluate your financial progress.

SPREADSHEET FLEXIBILITY

Because it is assumed that readers are already familiar with either Lotus 1-2-3 or Symphony, this book does not teach you how to use these programs. However, hundreds of examples of the Lotus commands and functions are demonstrated in the book. In addition, you will learn dozens of tips and techniques for spreadsheet design and development.

For example, the ability to change information is inherent in the design of the worksheets. Many of the planning models allow you to enter variable information into a worksheet via a parameter table. This technique makes it easy for you to change the assumptions in a worksheet and ask those "what if" questions which are so important to investors.

Appendix A also provides you with listings of the Lotus 1-2-3 cell formulas for some of the more complex worksheets. It also shows the keystrokes needed to set up the worksheets.

SAVE TIME AND ENERGY

To save you the effort of manually entering and checking the more than 60 sample worksheets, the publisher has made the Lotus 1-2-3 and Symphony models available on a floppy disk. The disk will allow you to start immediately on your personal financial plan. Instructions on how to use the disk and customize the worksheets also are available.

If there are any errors in the worksheets, we would appreciate your writing a brief description of the problem and any suggested solution. Suggestions for worksheet improvements or other models would also be appreciated. Please write to the author in care of: TAB Books, Inc. P.O. Box 40, Blue Ridge Summit, PA 17214.

SECTION 2

MONEY AND THE PERSONAL COMPUTER

Why Use a Microcomputer?

The personal computer is the newest wave of change in our society today. Nowhere is this change more evident than in the area of personal finance. In the past, only corporations and wealthy individuals could afford a professional planner. But today, as home computers become more numerous and users become more sophisticated and independent, they want to become more involved in their personal financial planning. More and more seek to use these professional tools to set personal financial goals.

THE POWER OF THE PC

A computer can make your life as an investor a lot easier. You can use it to set up your own tracking system tailored to your own investments. It can analyze enormous amounts of information. Within seconds, it can project the results in the form of a chart, table or graph, enabling you to size up an investment opportunity quickly and accurately.

Today's PC users can use the computer to customize their personal finances. They can create dozens of programs designed to help answer the hundreds of "what if" questions that are so important to an investor, such as:

- Where do I stand now?
- How can I get where I want to be?
- What is the actual return I'm getting on my investments?
- What effect will a 1 percent increase in the return on my investments make?
- What alternatives do I have and how do they stack up?
- What do I need to save to keep my income up with inflation?
- How much do I need to set aside each year so that I can have enough money for my kids to go to college?

DO YOU NEED A COMPUTER?

You don't necessarily need a computer to manage your finances. Almost anyone with a finan-

cial calculator probably could complete the worksheets in this book in a day or so. But it would be time-consuming and tedious and not nearly as flexible and useful as using a computer.

Another way would be to complete one of those standard, preprinted personal financial forms that you find in your local stationery store. But all of those standard forms have one drawback: they are not personal. I find them restrictive, complicated, and inflexible. Standard forms are usually made for financial planners—not for individual investors. They are designed so that planners can read them quickly. Most individual investors who fill out these forms leave lots of blank spaces in some areas and are forced to squeeze information into others.

Up until now you could not combine the best parts of one financial form with the best parts of another. That is, not until the personal computer gave you the ability to design your own financial worksheets. Now you can construct your financial reports to fit your own particular situation. You decide what's important because you're the one who has to use it.

Another important consideration is the microcomputer itself. While everything else keeps going up in price, the cost of computers keeps coming down. In 1955, a calculation that cost $14.54 and took 375 seconds to complete, today costs seven cents and takes less than one second. Computers are exciting. Spend a couple of hours sitting in a quiet place reading about computers and the future—it can be fun. I think you'll enjoy the exercises in this book. The worksheets have been designed with sincerity and humor. If you give it

your best effort, you will be rewarded with valuable information which you can use to make your investment more successful, and have some fun along the way.

CUSTOMIZING YOUR PERSONAL FINANCES

There are many home financial software packages available for sale today. Why, then, should you take the time to customize your own financial worksheets? The answer is threefold.

First, since investment portfolios differ, investors will always want special reports. No matter what your level of investment sophistication, using a customized computer worksheet can help you make better investment decisions.

If you find a personal financial software package that meets your needs, you should buy it. The value of this book would then be to enhance and embellish that software package without your having to hire a programmer. If you can't find a

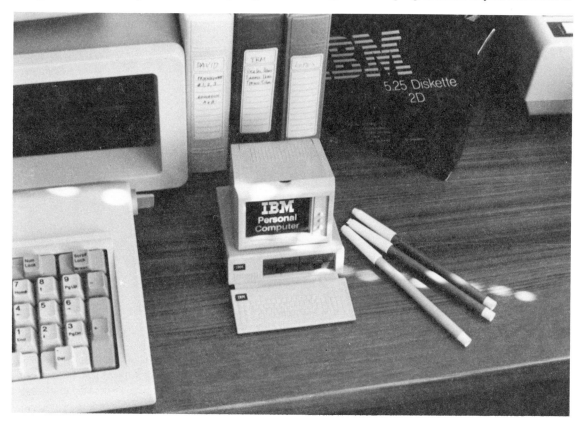

customized program, then this book will help you to personalize your investments.

Second, as your needs change over time, and your software package does not, this book will help you create new and different financial reports.

The third factor is cost. Good financial management software is not cheap. It could cost you from $200 to $500 for a comprehensive package, or over $500 for a hands-on training course in PCs and personal finance. But one report in this book can easily save you the cost of the book.

EVALUATING
FINANCIAL SOFTWARE PACKAGES

Before you decide to shoehorn your personal finances into some crackerjack software package, make sure you understand how it works and what it does. I have spent many hours trying to get various new software programs to run on my PC. All of these programs were advertised as being "user-friendly."

Some questions to consider when deciding whether to buy a financial software package are:

1. Does the package meet my personal requirements?

2. Does it do what I want and how well does it do it?

3. Does it do a lot of things I don't need or want?

4. Is it easy to change my worksheet as my needs change?

5. How much does the commercial package cost?

6. How does this compare to doing it myself?

7. Is the package simple to use?

HOW TO BUY A
COMPUTER TO MANAGE YOUR MONEY

What do you do if you don't own a computer but you want to buy one and use it for your home investment program?

Buying a computer for investing and personal finances doesn't mean running down to a computer

store and picking out the cheapest system or the most expensive one. The trip to the local computer store should be the last step in the process.

The first thing to do is get as much information as you can before you start looking for a computer. Buy a copy of a current computer magazine. Read about what's new and different. Become familiar with the terminology. Otherwise, once you walk into a computer store you will be overwhelmed by the jargon of hardware and software.

Try to get some hands-on experience before you purchase your own computer. Borrow a loaner from work or ask a friend who owns a computer for a demonstration. Try out a word processor or a spreadsheet program. You quickly will appreciate where and how to use a computer in your own home.

Then consider the way you now handle your personal finances. If you spend a lot of time reading and studying financial magazines and you spend hours each week preparing stock charts showing the volume and volatility of a few securities, a computer will save you a lot of time and improve the quality of your decisions.

Even if you are a relatively passive investor, a computer can still come in handy. It is a tool that can significantly reduce the amount of time required to make an investment decision. While it doesn't make the decisions for you, a computer will free you from the drudgery of pencil and eraser.

Required
Programs and Equipment

The worksheets in this book were first developed on an IBM Personal Computer using the Lotus 1-2-3 program, and then converted to the Symphony format on an IBM PC-AT. In their spreadsheet mode, the two programs look very much alike. Since the sample worksheets in this book were created using 1-2-3, the major emphasis will be on that product.

SYSTEM OVERVIEW

Most of the sample worksheets illustrated are simple and general enough that they can be created by almost any spreadsheet program—VisiCalc, SuperCalc, MultiPlan or whatever. My intent was to utilize and emphasize those spreadsheet functions which are most common to all spreadsheet programs. Therefore, most of the 1-2-3 commands used in this book will be familiar to users of other spreadsheet programs.

DESCRIPTION OF
HARDWARE REQUIREMENTS

The Lotus 1-2-3 worksheets were developed on an IBM Personal Computer with 256K of memory, two 320K disk drives, a monochrome display and the IBM Graphics Printer. The size of memory, the number of disk drives and the use of a hard disk can improve program operation and execution speed.

The 1-2-3 worksheets were converted to Symphony using an IBM PC-AT with 512K of memory, two double-sided disk drives (one with 1.2MB and one with 360K capacity), one 20MB fixed disk, a color monitor and an IBM Graphics Printer.

WHICH LOTUS PROGRAM IS RIGHT FOR YOU?

Lotus 1-2-3 and Symphony are both fully integrated software packages developed by Lotus Development Corporation. If your primary need is for spreadsheet analyses and graphics, 1-2-3 may be your choice. If you want to perform a lot of word processing, if you require extensive database functions and remote communications in addition to spreadsheet analysis, then Symphony could be your choice.

Symphony is a totally new product, not a

revamped or improved version of its predecessor, 1-2-3. Because it is so much more sophisticated than 1-2-3, Symphony is more difficult to master. Symphony has many more commands and menus than 1-2-3. This may frustrate the casual user, but will delight the more expert users who tend to demand more high-powered software, i.e., sophisticated integrated packages like Symphony.

LOTUS 1-2-3 AND SYMPHONY FEATURES

1-2-3 is big enough to handle most personal financial models. It is 2,048 rows by 256 columns. The minimum requirements to run 1-2-3 on the IBM PC are 192K RAM, MicroSoft DOS 1.1 or later version, and one double-sided, double-density disk. 1-2-3 will operate on the IBM PC, PC-XT, PC-AT, PCjr, Portable PC, or the IBM 3270 PC.

Symphony combines word processing, spreadsheet, communication, database, and graphics in-

to one integrated software package. This means that once information is entered, it is available to all Symphony functions. Symphony boasts the largest spreadsheet on the market, 8,192 rows by 256 columns, making it powerful enough to handle the most complex spreadsheet.

One of the nice features of Symphony is its windowing, which lets you control related or unrelated tasks at the same time on the same screen. With one keystroke, you can zoom the window to a full-size screen or overlay or display windows side by side.

Symphony will operate on the IBM PC, PC-XT, PC-AT or IBM Portable. Minimum requirements are 320K RAM, MicroSoft DOS 2.0 or later version, and two double-sided, double-density disks, or one floppy and one hard disk.

One important note: Lotus 1-2-3's formulas and data are upward compatible with Symphony, although Symphony is not downward compatible with 1-2-3.

USING LOTUS 1-2-3 AND SYMPHONY

Although this book discusses many Lotus 1-2-3 functions, it is not a substitute for the 1-2-3 manual. I assume that you have a basic understanding of the Lotus 1-2-3 and/or the Symphony spreadsheet programs. Before you begin using the worksheets in this book, take the time to read through the Lotus manual and tutorial programs until you are familiar with their commands and functions. The tutorials are well-written, interactive and simple to use. They are divided into several sections, and they take someone who has never before used a spreadsheet from the fundamentals of cursor movement all the way to advanced data management and graphing.

The Lotus programs include a HELP function.

If you forget a command or get confused about what to do next, you can press the F1 key and call up information and instructions about the command with which you are working.

In addition, Lotus Development Corporation maintains an 800 hot line service to assist their users and offers introductory and advanced courses designed to help you master Symphony and 1-2-3 functions.

THE USE OF GRAPHICS

Just as a picture is worth a thousand words, it follows that a graphic presentation of your worksheets will save a lot of time in evaluating your numbers. 1-2-3 and Symphony's graphics functions let you instantly create graphics and charts from information on your spreadsheet. You can change or update information on your worksheet and display a revised graph with a single keystroke.

1-2-3 and Symphony will function with a PC equipped with the monochrome monitor, but they cannot display charts and graphs before they are created on paper. A color/graphics adapter is needed for graphing functions. Because these worksheets were developed on a monochrome PC, graphics is not a major part of this book. Chapter 20 contains a discussion of how to print graphs on a matrix printer.

One last note: a graph should be used to complement, not take the place of, the worksheet numbers, since these numbers tend to give detail that a picture may not be able to show. More information about the use of graphics can be found in the appendices of the Symphony and 1-2-3 manuals.

SECTION 3

GETTING STARTED

How to Get Started

The worksheets in these chapters are an important part of this book. They are designed to give you a picture of your estate at a glance. Used properly, they can give you information which you can use to plan your finances. Don't just use them once and then forget them. You must keep them up to date. Personal money management is changing and dynamic. It is an ongoing job, but it will pay off in the end.

WHERE AND HOW TO BEGIN

The key to creating successful worksheets is knowing what information to present. Your worksheets should be carefully planned and tailored so that the important information comes across clearly. The important thing to remember when starting out is to keep it simple. Avoid the tendency to overwhelm; quality is more important than quantity.

If you are new to computers and spreadsheets, try constructing one of the easier reports first. My suggestion would be to begin with one of the Per-

sonal Inventory worksheets in Chapter 8.

If you are a sophisticated user, you might start with the Personal Financial Statement in Chapter 9. This is one of the more complex worksheets and actually contains three models within one spreadsheet. It is also the most important worksheet of all because it ties together every area of your financial investments.

Before you start to build a worksheet, take a close look at the examples in this book. Study them. Borrow from them. Feel free to copy the worksheets for your personal use. Use them as a guide to pencil out your version of a particular report. Don't worry about how crude it looks at first, or what you might have omitted. The beauty of a computer-generated report is that you can go back later and easily add, change, or delete entries in your worksheet. In fact, changes are expected. Your initial financial goals will be quite different from those of later years. Therefore, your worksheets will change over time.

Above all, don't get frustrated. It may take a

few attempts to get your personal finances on your computer, but it will be well worth it. What you want to end up with is a simple, personalized report, one that is easy to read and easy to use.

WORKSHEET DESIGN AND DEVELOPMENT

All the reports in this book fit on letter size 8 1/2-by-11-inch paper. The intent was to make all the worksheets simple, neat, and clear so that they can be easily read and understood.

As you create your own personal financial worksheets, I suggest that you file the reports in a three-ring binder. This will allow you to arrange the reports in any sequence you wish and to keep the information current. This notebook will be a valuable reference tool for you after you complete your worksheets.

Another suggestion is to go through your report binder with a highlighter pen and underline the important items in the reports—for example, your tax bracket, phone numbers, monthly or annual totals, etc. You can pencil in any new or additional information at any time. If you come across a new idea or modification to a worksheet, just punch three holes in it and insert it into your binder. Periodically you can go back through your notebook and update your worksheets.

Complicated spreadsheets should have instructions and explanatory notes built into the worksheet. A comment at the top of the worksheet could direct the user to a location where these notes and instructions are stored.

It is also a good practice to put the program name in the upper left-hand corner of your worksheet and use the 1-2-3 @TODAY function of display the date of your report in the upper right-

hand corner. These worksheet conventions will make it easy to remember the name of the report when you are looking at a printed copy months after you listed it out, and the date will make it simple to retain the most current copy of the report in your binder. You must remember, however, always to enter the current date when you first boot up your computer, or your report will not be dated correctly.

You can use the Lotus 1-2-3 @DATE function and RANGE command to enter and format the date. Date fields must be at least 10 characters wide in order to display month, day and year with the correct editing.

An easy way to key a series of dates down a column is to key in the first date using the @DATE command, and copy the date field down the column. Then go back and use the EDIT function to change each date field. To enter any given date, the @DATE function should be keyed as follows:

@DATE (year, month, day), e.g.,
@DATE(84,07,11)

SOME HELPFUL CUSTOMIZING TECHNIQUES

Many of the planning models in this book allow you to enter variable information via a parameter table. For example, suppose that you want to change the assumed inflation rate. If you simply change the inflation percentage in the assumptions table, 1-2-3 automatically will recompute the worksheet. Including a parameter table is a real timesaver and enhances the usability of a report. This technique makes it easier to vary the assumptions and allows you to learn the results of several strategies in a few seconds and then print only the best one.

When you first construct your spreadsheet, set it up as a single-space report; don't double space or insert blank lines and columns for easy readability. If you have these decorative blank rows, you cannot easily copy a formula down a column of a worksheet without having to go back and delete all the extra zeros that appear on the blank lines. In addition, the sort program will place all blank cells at the top of your report.

Remember, if you do put decorative dotted lines in your worksheet, they will make your spreadsheet larger. Putting dotted vertical lines in your program takes up as much memory as putting large numbers in each cell. You may be making your models unnecessarily large.

Many of the worksheets have the same format. For example, The Tax Model (Worksheet 13.2) and the Leverage Cash Flow before and after implementation (Worksheets 18.3 and 18.4) have a similar format. You can create this format once, put in the row and column headings and then store the format for future use. Thereafter, whenever you need to create a model with that format, you retrieve the format and plug in the new numbers.

The recalculation key (F9) can be quite useful. Each time you enter or change data in your spreadsheet, computations will be calculated automatically and quickly. However, when you are working on a large worksheet with many formulas and calculations, it may take some time for the worksheet to recalculate. One way to get around this problem is to change from automatic to manual recalculation. Then you can control the recalculation of the worksheet with the F9 key.

FORMATTING THE WORKSHEET

Formatting the worksheet output is very important. The maximum number of characters you can print on an 8 1/2-by-11 inch page is 135 characters, using compressed print on a dot matrix printer. This fact can help you make decisions about the length of labels and the width of columns. You might decide to enter numbers in thousands to save space, for example. To help you make formatting decisions, each worksheet in this book is preceded by the specifications that were used in its creation.

Report headings and column titles are best centered over alphabetical columns, but numeric field titles look best when right adjusted (i.e., all the way to the right). Numeric fields are usually formatted with commas, dollar signs and no decimals. The intent is to make all reports clear and simple so that they are easy to read and understand.

When printing your report, use the Margin option to set your left and right margins. If the worksheet does not fit on one page, try deleting some extraneous rows. If it wraps around because the report exceeds the paper width, try resetting your left margin to zero and increasing your right margin to 8 1/2 inches (i.e., 85).

If the report still doesn't fit, use the Compress Print option. This is accomplished by using the setup option under the /PRINT command. It passes a string of ASCII codes to your printer beginning with a backslash (\). All printers are different, so you should check the Lotus 1-2-3 manual to see what is required for your printer.

Don't forget to turn Compress Print off. Once Lotus 1-2-3 turns it on for a report, it will stay on for all succeeding reports until it is turned off. If you are not sure, check the status before printing, i.e., /WORKSHEET STATUS.

THE USE OF RANGE NAMES

It is a good idea to set up range names for different pages of areas within the same spreadsheet. This will make it easier and quicker to go between areas of your spreadsheet, and Lotus 1-2-3 automatically will expand the range when a new row is inserted.

One important point to remember is that if you insert a @SUM range that covers a specific group of values, any rows inserted later will be included only if they fall between the range coordinates. Get into the habit of inserting a row of hyphens as the last row of the range. Similarly, include the text column headings as the first coordinate of the range. Now the range will always be correct, no matter where you insert rows.

Ranges also are useful when you want to use parts of several models to build new ones. If you build consistency of cell ranges and labels into your models, for example, the worksheet title, name, and data can be extrapolated to a new worksheet using the File Combine and Add function without having to re-enter the data. Ranges are handy if you copy ratios or complex formulas from one model to another. This will save a lot of time building a new model.

INTEGRATING WORKSHEETS

Another advantage of using the range names feature is to assure you that you are working with the same pool of data when transferring information between worksheets. This ensures data integrity throughout your system.

Some of the models presented in this book are combined and integrated within one large spreadsheet program. This makes it easy to change information in one model and have it automatically update another model. For example, the Personal Financial Statement allows you to make changes to your supplementary schedules and automatically pass the information to the first page summary sheet.

Remember, however, that changes made to one part of the model, such as inserting and deleting rows and columns, can affect other parts of the worksheets. When any changes are made to the worksheet, the user should test the entire model with appropriate test data.

Most of the worksheets illustrated in this book are separate, stand-alone models. This makes it easy to construct the worksheets but puts the responsibility of maintaining the integrity of the data onto the user. Information that is common among worksheets must be, for the most part, entered separately. For example, your tax bracket is used in about 10 different models. Some people find it easier to simply rekey this number when it is required in a worksheet.

Others may want to integrate some of their separate models into one large spreadsheet. The worksheets presented in the chapters on Education, Asset Management, and Investments deal with areas that would lend themselves to and benefit from this type of integration.

BACKING UP THE WORKSHEETS

As you build your spreadsheet in the computer memory, periodically back up the program onto your disk. This will save you the trouble of having to redo everything in the event of a sudden power failure. Always make a backup copy of your disk at the end of your computer session. This will save

you hours of rework if the disk becomes defective.

Always have a supply of initialized disks handy to avoid being caught in the middle of a model with no space with which to save it. If you do find yourself caught in this way, however, remember that you can use any initialized disk in an emergency—even the DOS disk.

ADVANCED TOPICS—MACROS

One of 1-2-3's more advanced features is the ability to create keyboard macros. When used with the ALT key, any of the 26 letter keys can store a sequence of keystrokes that can represent a formula, a special command, or any other data string that might be used frequently. This macro capability is a useful tool for programming specific application. For example, 1-2-3 users often write macros to automate report printing or to handle file and graphic operations. For more information, refer to the Keyboard Macros section of 1-2-3 and Symphony's user's manual.

SPREADSHEETS ARE NOT INFALLIBLE

One final caution. Before you try to impress your family and friends with the skill of your worksheet analyses, you had better double check your formulas. Because formulas are not visible on the screen during calculation, users cannot see errors in their logic. If one formula is incorrect, many of the numbers in the worksheet also will be wrong. The larger and more complex the spreadsheet, the more likely it is that the problem will occur.

One solution to this problem is to build your model using the figures supplied in the sample worksheet. This will allow you to verify that your worksheet formulas are correct and that your totals match the totals in the sample worksheets. Then you can enter your own personal information, recalculate, print and save the worksheet.

Financial Goals

Personal finance can be a bewildering maze of rules of thumb, hot tips, and blind faith. To me, the key to sound personal financial management is planning. Once I accepted planning as an essential ingredient of my financial success, my wealth-building moved ahead at a much quicker pace.

BASIC INGREDIENTS OF PERSONAL FINANCE

The reason most people in this country do not achieve financial independence is that so few of them have specific financial goals. In addition, so few of them truly believe that these financial goals can become a reality. This is why I stress goals and why they are so important.

Financial goals should be both short range (1-3 years) and long range (five years or more). For example, a short-range goal might be a vacation in Europe. A long-range goal might be to become a doctor or purchase a home.

Begin by asking yourself what's important to you. Take a personal inventory. What do you want to accomplish with your life? What are your feelings toward money? Are you aggressive or conservative, or a little of each? Do you like saving every month or banking the bonus? Then establish priorities among your financial goals, because man's desires exceed his resources. Are there any goal conflicts, such as early retirement and a new car every three years?

Be realistic. Give yourself at least 5 years for long-term goals. Anything less may require a sacrifice of time, money, and energy so great that the price paid would not be worth the result.

Be specific. Goals should be measurable and have a specific date. And you must believe that you can achieve the goal by the deadline you have set.

Few people reach their financial goals in the ways they anticipated. But life has a way of working things out so that what seems impossible today will be routine tomorrow. With proper financial planning, you can make most of your dreams come true.

RANKING YOUR GOALS

Once you've decided on your goals, then you have to plan how you will achieve them. The next

WORKSHEET 6.1AB: RANKING YOUR GOALS

MARGINS: LEFT=3, RIGHT=85

COLUMNS: GLOBAL=10, A=20, B=15

FORMAT: COMMAS, NO DECIMALS

SORT BY: TERM WITHIN RANK

PRINTER: COMPRESS=OFF

RUN: AS NEEDED

HOUSE   22-Oct-84

WORKSHEET 6.1A: RANKING YOUR GOALS

GOALS	RANK	SHORT/LNG TERM	DAT NEEDED	AMOUNT NEEDED

E= ESSENTIAL   S= SHORT
I= IMPORTANT   L= LONG
N= NICE TO HAVE

BUY A HOUSE
BUY A VIDEO RECORDER
HAVE CHILDREN
BUY A SECOND CAR
BUY A NEW CAR
FINANCE EDUCATION
LARGE BANK ACOUNT
KIDS PRIVATE SCHOOL
START A BUSINESS
TENNIS LESSONS
EARLY RETIREMENT
FOREIGN TRAVEL
ANTIQUES/ART
COUNTRY CLUB
EXPENSIVE VACATION
NEW CARPET
SKI TRIPS
PAY OFF LOAN

WORKSHEET 6.1B   RANKING YOUR GOALS

GOALS	RANK	SHORT/LONG TERM	DATE NEEDED	AMOUNT NEEDED
	E= ESSENTIAL S= SHORT			
	I= IMPORTANT L= LONG			
	N= NICE TO HAVE			
START A BUSINESS	E	S	Jan-85	50,000
BUY A HOUSE	E	L	Jan-87	25,000
EARLY RETIREMENT	E	L	Jan-99	100,000
				$175,000
ANTIQUES/ART	I	S	Jan-85	3,000
HAVE CHILDREN	I	S	Jan-85	
KIDS PRIVATE SCHOOL	I	S	Jan-85	1,000
BUY A SECOND CAR	I	S	Jun-85	3,000
PAY OFF LOAN	I	L	Jan-95	7,500
FINANCE EDUCATION	I	L	Jan-95	40,000
				$54,500
TENNIS LESSONS	N	S	Jun-86	200
NEW CARPET	N	S	Jun-86	2,000
LARGE BANK ACCOUNT	N	S	Jan-85	5,000
BUY A NEW CAR	N	S	Jan-85	5,000
COUNTRY CLUB	N	S	Jan-85	500
BUY A VIDEO RECORDER	N	S	Jan-85	500
SKI TRIPS	N	S	Jan-86	500
FOREIGN TRAVEL	N	L	Jan-90	10,000
EXPENSIVE VACATION	N	L	Jun-87	2,000
				$25,700

worksheet will help you with this task. Start by typing in the heading information as shown in Worksheet 6.1A. Then key your goals randomly down column A as they occur to you, without any thought as to order. Don't fill in any other information; we'll go back and do that later.

After you have typed in all the goals you can think of, go back and rank your goals as Essential, Important or Nice to Have. Then use the 1-2-3 Sort Function to arrange your goals by rank as illustrated in Worksheet 6.1B. Next indicate whether your goals are short term or long term. Sort them again, this time by short /long term within rank. How do they look? Are your goals balanced between essential and not-so-essential, long term and short term?

Now estimate the date by which you want to achieve each goal and the amount of money required. An easy way to enter the date and amount fields is to key the first date and amount, format them using the RANGE command, then copy them down the rest of the columns. Then go back and

use the EDIT function to change each date and amount field to what you want it to be for that particular goal.

You may also want to sum the Money Needed column and calculate a subtotal by rank. However, this is optional since some of your goals, such as athletics or weight control, may not have an amount or date associated with them.

```
WORKSHEET 6.2:  EXAMPLE OF AN IRA AT AGE 22


MARGINS:   LEFT=5, RIGHT=85

COLUMNS:   GLOBAL=10, D=20,E=20

FORMAT:    COMMAS,NO DECIMALS

PRINTER:   COMPRESS=OFF
```

WORKSHEET 6.2:   EXAMPLE OF IRA AT AGE 22

AGE	INDIVIDUAL A	INDIVIDUAL B	FORMULA A	FORMULA B
22	2,240	0	2000*1.12	0
23	4,509	0	2000+B7*1.12	0
24	7,050	0	2000+B8*1.12	0
25	9,896	0	2000+B9*1.12	0
26	13,083	0	2000+B10*1.12	0
27	16,653	0	2000+B11*1.12	0
28	18,652	2,240	+B12*1.12	2000*1.12
29	20,890	4,509	+B13*1.12	2000+C13*1.12
30	23,397	7,050	+B14*1.12	2000+C14*1.12
31	26,204	9,896	+B15*1.12	2000+C15*1.12
32	29,349	13,083	+B16*1.12	2000+C16*1.12
33	32,871	16,653	+B17*1.12	2000+C17*1.12
34	36,815	20,652	+B18*1.12	2000+C18*1.12
35	41,233	25,130	+B19*1.12	2000+C19*1.12
36	46,181	30,146	+B20*1.12	2000+C20*1.12
37	51,723	35,763	+B21*1.12	2000+C21*1.12
38	57,929	42,055	+B22*1.12	2000+C22*1.12
39	64,881	49,101	+B23*1.12	2000+C23*1.12
40	72,667	56,993	+B24*1.12	2000+C24*1.12
41	81,387	65,832	+B25*1.12	2000+C25*1.12
42	91,153	75,732	+B26*1.12	2000+C26*1.12
43	102,092	86,820	+B27*1.12	2000+C27*1.12
44	114,343	99,239	+B28*1.12	2000+C28*1.12
45	128,064	113,147	+B29*1.12	2000+C29*1.12
46	143,431	128,725	+B30*1.12	2000+C30*1.12
47	160,643	146,172	+B31*1.12	2000+C31*1.12
48	179,920	165,713	+B32*1.12	2000+C32*1.12
49	201,511	187,598	+B33*1.12	2000+C33*1.12
50	225,692	212,110	+B34*1.12	2000+C34*1.12
51	252,775	239,563	+B35*1.12	2000+C35*1.12
52	283,108	270,311	+B36*1.12	2000+C36*1.12
53	317,081	304,748	+B37*1.12	2000+C37*1.12
54	355,130	343,318	+B38*1.12	2000+C38*1.12
55	397,746	386,516	+B39*1.12	2000+C39*1.12
56	445,476	434,898	+B40*1.12	2000+C40*1.12
57	498,933	489,085	+B41*1.12	2000+C41*1.12
58	558,805	549,776	+B42*1.12	2000+C42*1.12
59	625,861	617,749	+B43*1.12	2000+C43*1.12
60	700,965	693,879	+B44*1.12	2000+C44*1.12
61	785,080	779,144	+B45*1.12	2000+C45*1.12
62	879,290	874,641	+B46*1.12	2000+C46*1.12
63	984,805	981,598	+B47*1.12	2000+C47*1.12
64	1,102,981	1,101,390	+B48*1.12	2000+C48*1.12
65	1,235,339	1,235,557	+B49*1.12	2000+C49*1.12

THE VALUE OF INVESTING EARLY

The first 1-2-3 program I wrote dramatically demonstrates the value of investing early. It uses the example of an IRA, and shows that the earlier you start, the better off you'll be. The reason: you'll have a compound interest working for you tax free over a longer period. The example, which is illustrated along with the cell formulas in Worksheet

6.2, was written up in a financial newsletter and I adapted it to Lotus 1-2-3.

Two individuals, each 22, have an extra $2,000 a year to spend or invest as they choose. One opens an IRA, which averages 12 percent interest per year, and for six years he puts in $2,000 per year. He then stops contributing to his IRA, and for the next 37 years, spends the $2,000 on himself. The other individual does just the opposite. He spends his $2,000 a year on himself for six years and then, for the next 37 years, invests $2,000 a year in his IRA, which earns 12 percent per year. At age 65, both IRA's are worth the same amount!

This example dramatizes the power of time and money. Money is a machine that has the ability to work 24 hours a day, 365 days a year. When properly managed, it can be the nearest thing to perpetual motion, in that its return can compound to bring ever-greater returns.

To be a millionaire, you do not have to have much money, but you must start early and save, invest, and reinvest constantly. The earlier you start, the easier the goal. Success will take discipline, and you will have to tailor your lifestyle and financial planning while you are still young.

The earlier you start and the longer you hold to a sound financial plan, the more likely you will be to attain the lifestyle you want in your working years after retirement.

SECTION 4

FAMILY AND
FINANCIAL INFORMATION

Personal Information

Like most activities, personal financial management takes time and effort. In this chapter we will discuss various record keeping techniques which will provide you with the knowledge and experience to develop your own personal system.

RECORD KEEPING

For most people, the past is prologue. To know where you are going with your money, you first must know where you have been. Few, if any of us, are very successful with our personal finances unless we have all the necessary financial data in a proper and organized form. The gathering of this information is not the most exciting task, but skimming over this crucial first stage of organizing your personal finances could be a big mistake. It is as important to know exactly what your current financial profile looks like today as it is to know what you hope it to be tomorrow.

You should begin keeping records from your first job on through retirement. This can be a simple system—a file of various papers. But even if you're already well organized, the improved accuracy of a personal computer can help you compile your lists of personal information and maintain important dates and stored locations.

The worksheets in the next two chapters will assist you in arranging your personal records neatly, concisely and in one place. They will provide you with a practical guide for designing your own family information worksheets. Some of these reports are essential; others are optional. All should be kept in your three-ring binder, and other members of your family should know where they are located.

ONE FAMILY'S FINANCES

Most of the sample worksheets in this book are illustrated with the help of a hypothetical family, Mr. and Mrs. Somebody and their two children, Jill and Jack. This case study approach continues throughout the book and shows the interrelationship of all financial decisions.

James Somebody is 40 years old and a sales ex-

ecutive with SMC Corporation. His wife, Judy, is 38 years old and has her own decorating business. They were married 10 years ago and soon thereafter bought a $60,000 home. Within a year they had a daughter named Jill and three years later a son named Jack.

The Somebodys have a comfortable life. They own two late-model automobiles, a vacation cabin near a mountain lake, and a sailboat to use on their weekend retreats. They have some investments in stocks and bonds, and they have just purchased a home computer so that they can begin an investment program to finance a college education for their children and their own retirement at age 65.

Worksheet 7.1 provides vital information about Mr. and Mrs. Somebody such as social security

```
WORKSHEET 7.1:  FAMILY INFORMATION

MARGINS:  LEFT=5, RIGHT=85

COLUMNS:  GLOBAL=24

PRINTER:  COMPRESS=OFF

RUN:      AS NEEDED
```

WORKSHEET 7.1: FAMILY INFORMATION

	YOURSELF	YOUR SPOUSE
NAME	JAMES T. SOMEBODY	JUDY R. SOMEBODY
DATE OF BIRTH	OCT 18, 1944	MARCH 30, 1946
BIRTHPLACE	NEW YORK, NY	DES MOINES, IOWA
SOCIAL SECURITY NO.	222-34-7895	432-84-22324
DRIVER'S LICENSE	CALIF. D128756453	CALIF. B33987634
USA PASSPORT NO.	K12875-33	
MILITARY SERVICE	U.S. ARMY	
SERIAL NO.	US33459-98	
DATES OF SERVICE	JAN 1964 - DEC 1965	
EMPLOYER	SALES MARKETING CORP.	SELF-EMPLOYED
ADDRESS	EMBASSY TOWER	
CITY/STATE	ANYTOWN, USA 94111	
TELEPHONE	(456) 656-3456	
EMPLOYEE BENEFITS DEPT.	(456) 656-0393	
EMPLOYEE NO.	S-985567	
DATE HIRED	NOV. 6, 1974	
WILL - DATED	SEPT. 12, 1980	SEPT. 12, 1980
LOCATION	SAFE DEPOSIT BOX	SAFE DEPOSIT BOX
EXECUTOR OF ESTATE	TOM SULLIVAN	TOM SULLIVAN
	(456) 721-8411	(456) 721-8411
PREVIOUS MARRIAGE	NONE	NONE
NAME OF SPOUSE		
DATE TERMINATED		

CHILDREN		
NAME	1. JILL SOMEBODY	2. JACK SOMEBODY
ADDRESS	500 ALL-AMERICAN WAY	500 ALL-AMERICAN WAY
CITY/STATE	ANYTOWN,USA 94123	ANYTOWN,USA 94123
TELEPHONE	(456) 987-4321	(456) 987-4321
DATE OF BIRTH	MAY 20, 1975	SEPT. 23, 1978
BIRTHPLACE	ANYTOWN, USA	ANYTOWN, USA
SOCIAL SECURITY NO.	555-45-8732	556-23-0098
MARITAL STATUS	SINGLE	SINGLE

PARENTS	YOURS	YOUR SPOUSE'S
NAME	SAM & HARRIET SOMEBODY	JOHN & MARY STEVENS
ADDRESS	SEA BREEZE DRIVE	18 WHITTIER ST
CITY/STATE	BOCA RATON, FLA. 33003	DES MOINES, IOWA 56789
TELEPHONE	(809) 334-8765	(423) 345-8765
BIRTHPLACE-FATHER	NEW YORK, NY	PORTLAND, MAINE
BIRTHPLACE-MOTHER	NEW YORK, NY	DES MOINES, IOWA
MOTHER'S MAIDEN NAME	MORGAN	JOHNSTON

numbers, dates of birth, birthplaces, and driver's license numbers, as well as employer information. It also contains information about the Somebody's children and parents. You also might want to add your present address, your job title, the birthdates of your parents, or if they are deceased, their date of death.

The dotted vertical lines which appear in the next few worksheets are used to make the report more readable. They are entered by typing the character ":" into a one-position column.

FINANCIAL ADVISORS

Worksheets 7.2, 7.3 and 7.4 have similar formats, and they are designed so that each may easily be modified and expanded to fit your personal needs.

A quick way to construct these worksheets is to build the first unit or "box" of information with all its required formats, and copy that box down and/or across the worksheet as many times as it is required. Then go back and use the EDIT command to change the contents of the boxes.

There is no limit to the number of these miscellaneous financial advisor lists that you can construct, nor to what their design might be. You could have some which list business and professional associates, as well as old school contacts and relatives. Or you could record individual medical expenses for family members. One caution: some things are best done manually. There are times when trying to computerize all parts of your personal financial system may be more trouble than it's worth. It is simply not true that a computer can do everything better. Some parts of your money management system are best left to pad and pencil.

```
WORKSHEET 7.2:   INSURANCE INFORMATION


    MARGINS:   LEFT=5, RIGHT=85

    COLUMNS:   GLOBAL=20

    PRINTER:   COMPRESS=OFF

    RUN:       AS NEEDED
```

WORKSHEET 7.2:   INSURANCE INFORMATION

TYPE OF INSURANCE	LIFE	LIFE
NAME OF COMPANY	NEWSTATE	NEWSTATE
TELEPHONE	(456) 775-2349	(456) 775-2349
TYPE OF POLICY	TERM	TERM
POLICY NO.	B876-8723-8	AA8-3345-7
EFFECTIVE DATE	OCT 29, 1974	AUG 3, 1982
ANNUAL PREMIUM	$1,000	$500
LOCATION OF POLICY	SAFE DEPOSIT BOX	SAFE DEPOSIT BOX
FACE AMOUNT	$100,000	$50,000
OWNER	JAMES	JUDY
BENEFICIARY	JUDY	JILL & JACK
CASH VALUE		
AMOUNT BORROWED		

TYPE OF INSURANCE	HOMEOWNER'S	AUTOMOBILE
NAME OF COMPANY	GARDNERS	NEWSTATE
TELEPHONE	(456) 577-5499	(456) 775-2349
TYPE OF POLICY	DELUXE	COMP/COLLISION
POLICY NO.	BB98-756-76	AL-093365
EFFECTIVE DATE	MAY 14, 1984	JUNE 10, 1984
ANNUAL PREMIUM	$450	$1,100
LOCATION OF POLICY	FILE CABINET	FILE CABINET
FACE AMOUNT		
OWNER	JOINT	JOINT
BENEFICIARY		
CASH VALUE		
AMOUNT BORROWED		

TYPE OF INSURANCE	MEDICAL	DISABILITY
NAME OF COMPANY	SUPER MEDICAL	GOOD MUTUAL
TELEPHONE	(456) 475-1127	(456) 756-1129
TYPE OF POLICY	SALES MARKET GROUP	STANDARD
POLICY NO.	G-64756	DL-5567-9987
EFFECTIVE DATE	NOV. 6, 1974	JAN. 1, 1980
ANNUAL PREMIUM	COMPANY PAID	$500
LOCATION OF POLICY		FILE CABINET
FACE AMOUNT		
OWNER	JAMES	JAMES
BENEFICIARY	JUDY	JUDY
CASH VALUE		
AMOUNT BORROWED		

WORKSHEET 7.3:   BANKING INFORMATION

MARGINS: LEFT=5, RIGHT=85

COLUMNS: GLOBAL=25, A=20

PRINTER: COMPRESS=OFF

RUN: AS NEEDED

WORKSHEET 7.3:   BANKING INFORMATION

INSTITUTION:	NATIONAL BANK	COUNTRY BANK
ADDRESS:	SPEAR TOWER	CROSSROADS CENTER
CITY/STATE:	ANYTOWN, USA 94323	ANYTOWN, USA 94333
TELEPHONE NO:	(456) 555-9000	(456) 432-7667
TYPE OF ACCOUNT:	CHECKING	CHECKING
HELD BY:	JAMES	JUDY
ACCOUNT NO:	198748-76	20987-667
ATM CARD #:	ATM-998-987-21	ATM-888-987-33

INSTITUTION:	SOUTHERN CR UNION	STAGECOACH BANK
ADDRESS:	100 FLOWER STREET	400 14TH STREET
CITY/STATE:	ANYTOWN, USA 94323	ANYTOWN, USA 94333
TELEPHONE NO:	(456) 555-9567	(456) 432-2234
TYPE OF ACCOUNT:	CHECKING	SAVINGS
HELD BY:	JOINT	JOINT
ACCOUNT NO:	1123466543-0	889652209
ATM CARD #:		

INSTITUTION:	ANY S&L ASSOC	
ADDRESS:	CROSSROADS CENTER	
CITY/STATE:	ANYTOWN, USA 04333	
TELEPHONE NO:	(456) 432-2312	
TYPE OF ACCOUNT:	SAVINGS	
HELD BY:	JOINT	
ACCOUNT NO:	1-0559823	
SAFE DEPOSIT BOX:	BOX 123	

WORKSHEET 7.4: PERSONAL CONTACTS

MARGINS: LEFT=5, RIGHT=85

COLUMNS: GLOBAL=30

PRINTER: COMPRESS=OFF

RUN: AS NEEDED

CONTACTS   22-Oct-84

WORKSHEET 7.4:   PERSONAL CONTACTS

```
:==================================:==================================:
: ATTORNEY:                        : JAMES' DOCTOR:                   :
:                                  :                                  :
: ROBERT R. GLICK                  : ROBERT KENDELL                   :
: FRUMP,GLICK & FRUMP              : 36 CALIFORNIA ST                 :
: 5844 SPEAR BLVD SUITE 301        : ANYTOWN,USA 94999                :
: ANYTOWN, USA 94999               : (546) 755-0168                   :
: (546) 666-1772                   : ANSWERING SERVICE: (546) 775-3345 :
:                                  :                                  :
:==================================:==================================:
: ACCOUNTANT:                      : JUDY'S DOCTOR:                   :
:                                  :                                  :
: JERRY SPRINGER                   : STANLEY WHITE                    :
: SPRINGER TAX SERVICE             : 100 WILLOW RD                    :
: 35 - 34TH STREET NORTH           : ANYTOWN, USA 94999               :
: ANYTOWN, USA 94999               : (546) 439-7654                   :
: (546) 551-0119                   : ANSWERING SERVICE: (546) 349-4433 :
:                                  :                                  :
:==================================:==================================:
: STOCKBROKER:                     : CHILDREN'S DOCTOR:               :
:                                  :                                  :
: NANCY ADAMS                      : WILLIAM YEE                      :
: MERRILL LYNCH                    : 100 SALMON ST                    :
: TWO SECOND STREET SUITE 100      : ANYTOWN, USA 94999               :
: ANYTOWN, USA 94999               : (546) 743-8039                   :
: (546) 394-5400                   : ANSWERING SERVICE: (546) 746-0312 :
:                                  :                                  :
:==================================:==================================:
: FINANCIAL PLANNER:               : EXECUTOR:                        :
:                                  :                                  :
: CHUCK THOMAS                     : TOM SULLIVAN                     :
: BLOCK SECURITIES                 : 23 ELM DRIVE                     :
: 1020 SEQUEL ROAD                 : ANYTOWN,USA 94999                :
: ANYTOWN, USA 94999               : HOME: (546) 721-8411             :
: (546) 332-5434                   : WORK: (546) 765-0930             :
:                                  :                                  :
:==================================:==================================:
: REFERENCES:                      : REFERENCES:                      :
:                                  :                                  :
: BURT HOROWITZ                    : JUDY JOHNSON                     :
: 405 - 15TH AVENUE                : COLLEGE OF MUSIC                 :
: ANYTOWN, USA 94999               : ANYTOWN, USA 95442               :
: HOME (546) 898-2725              : HOME (546) 445-2084              :
: WORK (546) 896-3453              : WORK (546) 211-3122              :
:                                  :                                  :
:==================================:==================================:
```

Miscellaneous Information

If something happened to you, could your spouse or another close relative find all the forms, certificates and information needed to take care of your financial affairs? Chances are that you are the only one who knows where all your important papers are and where all your assets are invested.

EMERGENCY FILE

If this is true, you should take the time to complete the following two worksheets. They will make it easy for anyone to take care of your personal finances if you die or become seriously incapacitated.

The Letter of Last Instruction listed in Worksheet 8.1 is often a more appropriate place than your will for instructions concerning the details of your burial. This document is normally kept at home where it can be readily available in time of need. Be sure your executor knows where it is located.

You should also make two copies of Worksheet 8.1 and 8.2, one for yourself and the other for your spouse.

```
WORKSHEET  8.1:  DOCUMENT INFORMATION & LOCATION

MARGINS:  LEFT=5, RIGHT-85

COLUMNS:  A=30, B=30

PRINTER:  COMPRESS=OFF

RUN:      AS NEEDED
```

```
WORKSHEET  8.1:   DOCUMENT INFORMATION & LOCATION
----------------------------------------------------------------------
ITEM DESCRIPTION                 ¦ LOCATION
======================================================================
                                 ¦
ADOPTION PAPERS                  ¦ FILE CABINET
ALL CANCELLED BANK CHECKS        ¦ BASEMENT STORAGE
AUTO OWNERSHIP CERTIFICATE       ¦ SAFE DEPOSIT BOX
BANK BOOKS                       ¦ TOP DESK DRAWER
BIRTH CERTIFICATES               ¦ STRONG BOX
BURIAL INFORMATION               ¦ TOP DESK DRAWER
CHURCH RECORDS                   ¦ FILE CABINET
CITIZENSHIP PAPERS               ¦
COIN COLLECTION                  ¦ SAFE DEPOSIT BOX
CREDIT CARDS                     ¦ TOP DESK DRAWER
CREDIT RECORDS                   ¦ FILE CABINET
DEGREES, DIPLOMAS                ¦ FILE CABINET
DIVORCE RECORDS                  ¦
EMPLOYEE BENEFIT INFORMATION     ¦ FILE CABINET
EMPLOYEE'S HANDBOOK              ¦ FILE CABINET
FINANCIAL RECORDS                ¦ TOP DESK DRAWER
HOME IMPROVEMENT RECORDS         ¦ FILE CABINET
HOUSEHOLD INVENTORY              ¦ SAFE DEPOSIT BOX
INCOME TAX RECORDS               ¦ FILE CABINET
INSURANCE POLICIES               ¦ FILE CABINET
LETTER OF LAST INSTRUCTION       ¦ TOP DESK DRAWER
LICENSES & PERMITS               ¦ FILE CABINET
MARRIAGE CERTIFICATE             ¦ FILE CABINET
MEDICAL RECORDS                  ¦ FILE CABINET
MILITARY RECORDS                 ¦ FILE CABINET
NEGATIVES OF PERSONAL PROP       ¦ SAFE DEPOSIT BOX
OTHER RECORDS                    ¦
PERSONAL RESUME                  ¦ FILE CABINET
PICTURES OF PERSONAL PROP        ¦ FILE CABINET
POWER OF ATTORNEY                ¦ ATTORNEY: ROBERT GLICK
PRE & POSTNUPTIAL AGGREMENT      ¦ SAFE DEPOSIT BOX
PRIOR YEAR'S TAX FORMS           ¦ BASEMENT STORAGE
REAL ESTATE PAPERS               ¦ SAFE DEPOSIT BOX
SAFE DEPOSIT BOX                 ¦ FIRST S&L ASSOCIATION
SAFE DEPOSIT KEY                 ¦ TOP DESK DRAWER
SOCIAL SECURITY RECORDS          ¦ FILE CABINET
STOCK & BOND CERTIFICATES        ¦ SAFE DEPOSIT BOX
WARRANTIES & GUARANTEES          ¦ BASEMENT STORAGE
WILLS:  JAMES & JUDY             ¦ ATTORNEY: ROBERT GLICK
```

SAFE DEPOSIT BOX

Most people don't know all the items in their safe deposit box. When was the last time you put something in your safe deposit box? Can you name all the items in your box? Do you have a list?

This next worksheet will help you keep track

of the contents of your safe deposit box and assist you if you have to maintain a similar list for an elderly relative.

HOME IMPROVEMENT RECORD

Worksheet 8.3 will help you to record and remember all improvements made to your home. For tax purposes, you must separate maintenance and repair costs from capital improvements. Permanent improvements such as installing a patio or a new roof or furnace are capital expenditures and are added to the cost basis of your house.

As a rule of thumb, you capitalize (that is, depreciate rather than expense) large items or improvements that extend the useful life of the property. Worksheet 8.7 has some typical examples.

```
WORKSHEET  8.2:   CONTENTS OF SAFE DEPOSIT BOX



    MARGINS:   LEFT=5, RIGHT =85

    COLUMNS:   A=30, B=30

    PRINTER:   COMPRESS=OFF

    RUN:       AS NEEDED
```

```
SAFEBOX                                        22-Oct-84

WORKSHEET  8.2:  CONTENTS OF SAFE DEPOSIT BOX

              ANY SAVINGS AND LOAN ASSOC
              CROSSROADS CENTER
                  BOX 123
----------------------------------------------------------------
ITEM                          : DESCRIPTION
================================================================
                              :
AUTO OWNERSHIP CERTIFICATE     : 1983 VAN & 1979 BLUE HAWK
COIN COLLECTION                : SEE RARE COIN LIST
NEGATIVES OF PERSONAL PROP     : DATED JUNE 15, 1983
DEED TO HOME                   : DEED & SALES CONTRACT
MORTGAGE DOCUMENTS             : FINANCIAL CORPORATION
TITLE INSURANCE POLICY         : FIDELITY WEST
DEED TO VACATION CABIN         : DEED & SALES CONTRACT
MORTGAGE DOCUMENTS             : BLUE LAKE S & L
TITLE INSURANCE POLICY         : SOUTH COAST TITLE
US TREASURY NOTES              : CERTIFICATE NO.'S 11223-11234
MUTUAL FUND                    : JAZY GROWTH FUND
STOCK CERTIFICATES             : NXXON OIL - 100 SHARES
STOCK CERTIFICATES             : GLOBAL OIL CO - 100 SHARES
STOCK CERTIFICATES             : SMC COPRORATION - 200 SHARES
```

If you are in doubt about a particular item, ask your tax advisor.

PREPARING YOUR HOME FOR SALE

You also can use Worksheet 8.3 when you sell your home. If you want to sell your home as quickly as possible and at the best possible price, it may be worth spending some money putting the house in the best possible condition to attract buyers. You are allowed to deduct any fix up expenses which make your house salable, such as wallpapering, painting and other similar repairs from any profit you realize.

In order to qualify, these repairs must be made within 90 days prior to the sale of the house and be paid no later than 30 days after the date of the sale.

HOUSEHOLD INVENTORY

Worksheet 8.4 may take you a few hours to complete, but it will transform what is now probably utter chaos into a semblance or order.

Begin by going through every room in your house and listing each item of worth. Besides describing each item, you should include its age and original price. In some categories of property, such

---

```
WORKSHEET  8.3:   CAPITAL IMPROVEMENT RECORD


    MARGINS:    LEFT=5, RIGHT=85

    COLUMNS:    GLOBAL=10, B=15, C=30, D=10

    PRINTER:    COMPRESS=OFF

    RUN:        AS NEEDED
```

```
IMPROVE                                           22-Oct-84

WORKSHEET  8.3:   CAPITAL IMPROVEMENT RECORD
```

DATE	COMPANY	DESCRIPTION OF LABOR & SUPPLIES	AMOUNT
01-Jan-76	SCHILLER	COPPER PLUMBING (UPSTAIRS)	2,500
22-Feb-77	CHAN & SONS	NEW ROOF	1,500
08-Jun-78	CITY GLASS	ALUMINUM WINDOWS (REAR)	450
03-Nov-79	HANCOCK ELEC	ELECTRICAL WIRING (UPSTAIRS)	500
11-Mar-80	BAY CONSTR CO	SCREEN PATIO & SLAB	3,200
02-Sep-80	BAY CONSTR CO	PATIO FENCE	400
17-Aug-81	BEST HEATING	NEW FURNANCE	950
05-Oct-81	HOME SUPPLY	NEW 50 GAL WATER HEATER	450
11-Jan-82	SEARS	NEW WALL-TO-WALL CARPET	1,500
22-Apr-82	SUN POOLS	SWIMMING POOL	5,700
24-Dec-83	DECORATE	MINI BLINDS (UPSTAIRS)	600
09-Aug-84	GEORGE BURTON	REMODEL KITCHEN CABINETS	825

```
                                                  $18,575
```

WORKSHEET 8.4: HOUSEHOLD INVENTORY

MARGINS: LEFT=3, RIGHT=85

COLUMNS: GLOBAL=11, A=20, B=30

FORMAT: COMMAS, $, NO DECIMALS

SORT BY: ORIGINAL VALUE

PRINTER: COMPRESS=OFF

RUN: AS NEEDED

HOUSE   22-Oct-84

WORKSHEET 8.4: HOUSEHOLD INVENTORY

ITEM	DESCRIPTION	DATE PURCHASED	ORIGINAL VALUE
COMPUTER	HOME COMPUTER & ACCESSORIES	12-Jan-83	3,000
COIN COLLECTION	SEE RARE COIN LIST	01-Mar-70	1,700
CLOTHES	OURS AND THE KIDS		1,200
LIVING ROOM	DRAPES AND CARPET	02-Jun-75	1,025
KITCHEN	BESTMORE REFRIGERATOR	02-Jun-75	850
KITCHEN	BESTMORE GAS RANGE	02-Jun-75	750
DINING ROOM	DINING SET	02-Jun-75	710
TELEVISION/RADIOS	GCA REMOTE/TONY PORTABLE	12-May-80	700
PIANO	TAMAHA — UPRIGHT	26-Aug-84	600
BEDROOMS	TWO QUEEN SIZE BEDS/LAMPS	02-Jun-75	520
LIVING ROOM	MODULAR SOFA	02-Jun-75	515
LIVING ROOM	ORIENTAL RUG	17-Dec-83	450
ANTIQUES	MOM'S TABLE IN HALL		425
STEREO SET	GITSUBISHI'S WITH VCR	02-Jun-75	425
KITCHEN	QUICK RINSE DISHWASHER	02-Jun-75	400
LIVING ROOM	BEAUMONT LOVE SEAT	02-Jun-79	380
LIVING ROOM	BLUE WING CHAIR	02-Jun-75	375
PAINTINGS	CALDER PRINT	14-Nov-83	350
SILVER	CUSTOM SILVER SET	02-Jun-76	325
BEDROOMS	CERAMIC LAMPS AND DESK	02-Jun-82	325
CAMERA EQUIPMENT	TIKKON 35MM	01-Jan-81	300
LAWN FURNITURE	TABLE & FOUR CHAIRS	02-Jun-75	250
JEWELRY	WEDDING RING	28-Feb-79	225
EXPENSIVE TOOLS	ELECTRIC SAW/DRILL/ETC	12-Mar-77	200

TOTAL ORIGINAL VALUE = $16,000

as clothing, you may wish to lump together a number of articles.

You might also want to include notes and comments about certain valued objects, such as serial numbers. You might even design a special form for them. For example, items of sentimental value might have considerable worth to you and your family: mementos, family heirlooms, photo albums, etc. All of these can be organized, catalogued and sorted in a form designed to meet your own needs.

It is important to note that although it may take a while to compile this list, the accuracy and completeness of this information will be of great assistance when looking at your overall financial situation.

A computer list not only will ensure that your list is complete, but it also helps to assure you of smooth claims processing. Insurance agents are less likely to question claims based on such inventory lists, especially when they are printed by a computer. A copy of this worksheet should be placed in your insurance folder.

You also can use a modification of this worksheet to list and manage any collectibles you have in your home, such as gems, stamps, rare books, etc. The next worksheet shows an example of how to organize a rare coin collection on a worksheet.

COLLECTING FOR PROFIT

There are many benefits to using your personal computer in conjuction with your hobby, whether it be collectibles, club membership lists, or a PTA fund drive. You can save hundreds of hours of sorting, updating, and printing, which frees you up to spend more time doing the creative aspects of your hobby.

Maintaining information about your hobby, it would seem, can be done by hand just as easily as on a computer. So why go to the trouble of using a computer? Like almost any computer application, the initial data entry is not any easier than listing by hand. But once it's done, you don't have to do it again. The information can be retrieved, sorted, and listed out in a variety of ways.

Collecting also provides the dual satisfaction of a hobby and an investment. If you intend to invest seriously in a hobby, you can use your computer to keep track of your collectibles. Stamp collecting and rare coins, for example, have always been popular as a hobby, but only recently have they been taken seriously as an investment. Some investors who are concerned about a renewed inflation are reluctant to put all their savings and investment capital into paper instruments. Investors like to see and handle real wealth, i.e., hard assets like gold and silver. In the past 10 years, for example, U.S. coins have ranked as the No. 1 investment with a compounded annual rate of return of more than 10 percent per year.

Whether your collection specializes in a particular time period or geographical location, or you collect randomly from various areas and periods, a PC can help you track price changes, total return on your investment, and future purchases.

Mr. Somebody has been collecting gold coins for the past 15 years, and although he doesn't have very many coins, the ones he does collect are of the highest quality. Worksheet 8.5 is a listing of his gold coin collection. It has a description of the coins he owns as well as the ones he is following and would like to own. It shows the quantity, date and cost of the coins he purchased, the gold content of the coins in troy ounces, its intrinsic value based on the current price of gold, a recently quoted price for the coins, the percent by which the recent price exceeds the intrinsic value, the current market value and the percent return.

RECORDING AUTOMOBILE EXPENSES

All expenses for operation of a vehicle for business purposes are tax deductible. You have a choice of either deducting the actual operating costs of your car during business trips or deducting a flat IRS allowance based on the business mileage

```
WORKSHEET  8.5:  MANAGING COLLECTIBLES

MARGINS:   LEFT=5, RIGHT=136

COLUMNS:   GLOBAL = 10, A=22, B=5

FORMAT:    DOLLARS AND SENSE

PRINTER:   COMPRESS=ON

SORT BY:   COIN DESCRIPTION, ASCENDING

RUN:       AS NEEDED
```

WORKSHEET 8.5: MANAGING COLLECTIBLES

PRICE OF GOLD PER OUNCE: $345.00

AS OF   18-Oct-84

COIN DESCRIPTION	QTY	DATE PURCHASED	COST	GOLD CONTENT	INTRINSIC VALUE	RECENT PRICE	PREMIUM PERCENT	MARKET VALUE	PERCENT RETURN
AUSTRIAN 100-CORONA	0			0.9802	338.17	346.00	2.32%	0.00	
BRITISH SOVEREIGN	0			0.2350	81.07	94.00	15.94%	0.00	
CANADIAN MAPLE LEAF	1	22-Jan-84	360.00	1.0000	345.00	366.00	6.09%	366.00	1.67%
MEXICAN 50-PESO	0			1.2057	415.97	447.00	7.46%	0.00	
MEXICAN COINS									
ONE OUNCE	1	04-Feb-80	312.00	1.0000	345.00	367.00	6.38%	367.00	17.63%
ONE-HALF OUNCE	0			0.5000	172.50	188.00	8.99%	0.00	
ONE-QUARTER OUNCE	0			0.2500	86.25	98.00	13.62%	0.00	
SO. AFRICAN KRUGERRAND									
ONE OUNCE	2	12-Oct-75	200.00	1.0000	345.00	366.00	6.09%	732.00	266.00%
ONE-HALF OUNCE	1	12-Oct-75	100.00	0.5000	172.50	190.00	10.14%	190.00	90.00%
ONE-QUARTER OUNCE	0			0.2500	86.25	99.00	14.78%	0.00	
ONE-TENTH OUNCE	0			0.1000	34.50	42.00	21.74%	0.00	
US DOUBLE EAGLE ($20)									
ST GAUDENS	1	17-Nov-79	500.00	0.9675	333.79	760.00	127.69%	760.00	52.00%
LIBERTY (TYPE I)	0			0.9675	333.79	1,300.00	289.47%	0.00	
LIBERTY (TYPE II)	0			0.9675	333.79	675.00	102.22%	0.00	
LIBERTY (TYPE III)	0			0.9675	333.79	647.50	93.99%	0.00	
US EAGLE ($10)									
INDIAN HEAD	0			0.4838	166.91	625.00	274.45%	0.00	
LIBERTY (NM)	0			0.4838	166.91	800.00	379.30%	0.00	
LIBERTY (WM)	1	02-Jan-77	150.00	0.4838	166.91	337.25	102.05%	337.25	124.83%
US HALF EAGLE ($5)									
INDIAN HEAD	0			0.2419	83.46	552.50	562.03%	0.00	
LIBERTY (NM)	0			0.2419	83.46	585.00	600.97%	0.00	
LIBERTY (WM)	1	01-Aug-81	125.00	0.2419	83.46	226.00	170.80%	226.00	80.80%
	8		$1,747.00					$2,978.25	70.48%

traveled during the year.

If you decide to keep track of actual expenses you should record all vehicle expenses as they occur. These include gas, oil, lubrication, maintenance, repairs, insurance,parking, tools, license, and registration fees. The purchase price of the vehicle and major repairs can not be expensed, but must be depreciated over the life of the vehicle.

Keeping itemized records for your car and/or truck is tedious work. One way to ease the pain is to have a notebook in the business vehicle so that you can record each fill-up and every oil change. You also may want to include repairs and accessories, tire mileage, and a trip diary which would note the business purpose of the trip, clients visited, and any additional expenses.

The vehicle record could later be transcribed to a spreadsheet like Worksheet 8.6. It shows all the information about the vehicle and computes total cost and miles per gallon.

```
WORKSHEET  8.6:   GAS AND OIL CONSUMPTION


MARGINS:   RIGHT=5, LEFT=75

COLUMNS:   GLOBAL=10

FORMAT:    DOLLARS AND SENSE

PRINTER:   COMPRESS=OFF

RUN:       AT LEAST ONCE-A-MONTH
```

WORKSHEET 8.6: GAS AND OIL CONSUMPTION

VEHICLE = 1984 TOYOTA TRUCK

DATE	SPEEDOMETER READING	GALLONS	COST	MILES PER GALLON	OIL/LUB COST
10-Apr-84	7	13.2	0.00	22.0	1.05
16-Apr-84	297	9.8	15.50	33.6	
21-Apr-84	626	10.9	17.34	27.4	
27-Apr-84	925	9.1	13.50	34.6	
04-May-84	1,240	11.0	17.15	28.9	1.05
10-May-84	1,558	10.2	14.79	32.1	
16-May-84	1,885	11.0	16.05	26.9	
20-May-84	2,181	10.9	16.40	30.2	
26-May-84	2,510	11.3	18.15	31.4	1.05
01-Jun-84	2,865	11.7	18.00	27.9	
09-Jun-84	3,192	10.9	16.79	29.7	1.85
16-Jun-84	3,516	8.7	16.52	22.0	
18-Jun-84	3,707	10.6	9.51	31.6	1.05
23-Jun-84	4,042	11.8	18.67	26.0	
02-Jul-84	4,349	10.6	16.00	32.7	
06-Jul-84	4,696	11.0	16.52	28.9	12.47
12-Jul-84	5,014	10.5	15.74	30.1	1.05
17-Jul-84	5,330	10.7	16.01	32.6	
23-Jul-84	5,679	11.4	17.02	27.3	
26-Jul-84	5,990	10.7	16.01	28.8	
31-Jul-84	6,298	10.8	16.00	30.6	
05-Aug-84	6,629	11.1	16.72	28.9	1.05
10-Aug-84	6,950	11.3	16.56	26.4	
15-Aug-84	7,248	3.2	5.00	36.9	
17-Aug-84	7,366	11.4	16.92	28.9	
22-Aug-84	7,695	11.4	17.02	24.5	1.05
26-Aug-84	7,974	9.9	14.75	32.4	
31-Aug-84	8,295	10.8	16.65	30.6	
02-Sep-84	8,626	3.2	5.00	29.4	
04-Sep-84	8,720	11.0	16.50	29.6	1.05
08-Sep-84	9,046	3.3	5.00	22.7	
09-Sep-84	9,121	10.2	14.18	31.8	
13-Sep-84	9,445	10.7	15.85	28.5	
17-Sep-84	9,750	10.5	15.77	30.4	1.05
22-Sep-84	10,069	11.1	16.51	30.0	
25-Sep-84	10,402	11.3	17.43	32.0	13.47
01-Oct-84	10,764				
TOTALS =			$531.53	27.9	$37.24

Personal Financial Statement

Preparing your own personal financial statement on your home computer is easy once you understand the logic and the language. It also can be one of your most valuable financial planning tools.

WHAT ARE YOU WORTH?

A personal financial statement has two parts: the *balance sheet* and an *income and expense statement*. One asks the question "What is my net worth?" The other asks "Where does my money go?"

The balance sheet, or new worth statement as it is sometimes called, is a snapshot of where you stand financially at any given point in time. It is the difference between your assets (what you own), and your liabilities (what you owe).

Why go to all the trouble of calculating your net worth? Because it is essential for any sound investment program. Anyone who is able to invest some money—no matter how small the amount—should plan his or her own financial future. To do this effectively, potential investors should have a clear picture of their financial profile.

MONEY MATTERS

To begin, calculate as accurately as possible the market value of your property, your home, autos, investments. How do you find out what things are worth? You can use the previous chapter's worksheets as a starting as a starting point, then check your local newspaper for advertisements for comparable homes and autos. Your daily newspaper also will tell you what your stocks, bonds, money market accounts and mutual funds are worth. If you own an unlisted investment trust, oil, and gas limited partnerships), check the latest annual report for the current value of the asset. If that's not possible, value the asset at its cost.

Now for liabilities, start with all current bills, credit cards, etc. Next list the unpaid balance on your home, car, vacation vehicles, etc. Total the assets column, then the liabilities column. Subtract your liabilities from your assets. The result is your net worth.

CONSTRUCTING THE NET WORTH MODEL

The personal financial statement is divided into two parts. The first page, Worksheet 9.1, summarizes all the information which is found on the supplementary schedules, Worksheet 9.2. You may have as many supplementary schedules as you like. Using a spreadsheet will make it easy to tie the supplementary totals back to your summary page.

You will be constructing your own personal financial statement vertically down your spreadsheet, with the first page at the top of your spreadsheet and all supplementary schedules following below. This format will allow you maximum flexibility.

I recommend that you double space between the major categories on the first page of your personal financial statement, and that you allow yourself lots of room to make it easy to read. I also suggest that titles and heading information be entered in capital letters, and that all detail information be in lowercase letters.

Next enter the titles of your assets and liabilities, and their amounts. You might want to put in assets and liabilities which you expect to have later on, but don't have now, such as education loans. Don't worry if part of your spreadsheet moves off the screen. We'll come back later and adjust it to make sure it prints on a single page. Try to line up related assets and liabilities. For example, when you enter real estate assets, cross over and enter mortgages. This provides a nice touch and makes your statement easier to read.

Total your assets and liabilities using the @SUM Function, then put the cursor in the NET WORTH cell and enter your formula for net worth (i.e., NET WORTH = ASSETS – LIABILITIES). Go back and test your spreadsheet by changing your assets and liabilities amounts to make sure that your net worth is correctly recalculated.

Now we are ready to work with the bottom half of the first page of your personal financial statement. Enter your ANNUAL SOURCES OF INCOME, PERSONAL INFORMATION, CONTINGENT LIABILITIES, and GENERAL INFORMATION. As you enter this information across several cells, remember to type it in as one long field and line it up afterward in EDIT Mode. If you have contingent liabilities, you may require a separate schedule with some additional information. Allow room at the bottom for at least two signatures and a date.

Make any cosmetic changes necessary in order to make your statement look better. Remember, someday an experienced loan officer will be scrutinizing this statement, and first impressions count.

```
WORKSHEET 9.1:   PERSONAL FINANCIAL STATEMENT


MARGINS:    LEFT=3, RIGHT=85

COLUMNS:    GLOBAL=12

FORMAT:     COMMAS, NO DECIMALS

PRINTER:    COMPRESS=OFF, RANGE NAME=SMT

RUN:        SEMI-ANNUALLY
```

```
WORKSHEET  9.1:  PERSONAL FINANCIAL STATEMENT
---------------------------------------------------------------------------
         PERSONAL FINANCIAL STATEMANT ... AS OF ...   22-Oct-84

         JAMES T. SOMEBODY                500 ALL-AMERICAN WAY
         JUDY R. SOMEBODY                 ANYTOWN, USA  94123
                                          (465) 987-4321
===========================================================================
    ASSETS       :     AMOUNT    : :   LIABILITIES    :    AMOUNT
 --------------------------------------------------------------------------
CASH                             : :  CURRENT BILLS
   Checking accounts     1,000   : :     Mortgage or rent          550
   Savings accounts      5,000   : :     Charge accts              150
   Money-market funds    2,000   : :     Credit cards            1,250
   Life insurance cash val       : :     Other bills
                                 : :
MARKETABLE SECURITIES            : :  LOANS
   Stocks               6,500    : :     Auto                    5,000
   Bonds                         : :     Education
   Gov't securities      3,000   : :     Sailboat                5,000
   Mutual funds                  : :     Other
                                 : :
NON-LIQUID INVESTMENTS           : :  MORTAGES
   Real estate: home   110,000   : :     Home                   30,000
   Other properties     35,000   : :     Vacation property      21,000
   IRA or KEOGH          5,500   : :     Other properties
   Equity in business            : :
                                 : :
PERSONAL PROPERTY                : :  TAXES DUE
   Automobiles          12,000   : :     Federal                 3,000
   Household furniture  15,000   : :     State                       0
   Collectibles          1,000   : :     Local
   Other                 5,500   : :     Other
                                 : :
TOTAL ASSETS           201,500   : :  TOTAL LIABILITIES          65,950
                                 : :
                                 : :  NET WORTH                 135,550
===========================================================================
      ANNUAL SOURCES OF INCOME   : :       PERSONAL INFORMATION
 --------------------------------------------------------------------------
SALARY: James          31,000    : :  OCCUPATION                   AGE
BUS. INCOME: Judy      15,000    : :
OTHER INCOME            1,000    : :  James: Executive              40
INTEREST                  300    : :
DIVIDENDS                 400    : :  Judy: Decorator               38
                                 : :
TOTAL INCOME           47,700    : :  MINOR CHILDREN: 2       6 AND 10
===========================================================================
      CONTINGENT LIABILITIES     : :        GENERAL INFORMATION
 --------------------------------------------------------------------------
AS ENDORSER OR CO-MAKER?      No : :  ANY ASSETS PLEDGED?            No
                                 : :  DEFENDENT IN ANY SUITS?        No
                                 : :  EVER TAKEN BANKRUPTCY?         No
===========================================================================
THE UNDERSIGNED CERTIFIES THAT THE INFORMATION HEREIN IS TRUE
AND ACCURATE AS OF THIS DATE.

DATE _____              SIGNATURE _____
                                    SIGNATURE _____
```

SUPPLEMENTARY SCHEDULES

You are now ready to construct your supplementary schedules. To begin, use the COPY command to copy down the heading information from the top of your first page to cell location **A100**. Then use the EDIT key to change the headings to read SUPPLEMENTARY SCHEDULE.

Schedule A should contain all your cash and banking information, including savings and loan associations, credit unions and money market accounts. I like to include account numbers because it allows for quick reference when a loan officer needs to check the current status of an account.

Enter your formula for TOTAL CASH ON HAND and note the cell numbers for the individual categories of cash. Now go back to your first page and enter those cell numbers in the corresponding row and column (e.g., for checking accounts enter

+G110+G111). The correct amounts should appear on your first page. If not, go back to Schedule A and check the number of the cell that contains the particular amount in question.

Continue working your way down the supplementary schedule, always noting the cell that contains the category amount and entering that cell number on the corresponding line on your first page. Now your financial statement will automatically crossfoot to your detailed supplementary schedules. Remember to stop and SAVE your spreadsheet after completing each individual schedule.

When you finish, print your supplementary schedule to make sure it all fits on one page. If not, simply divide it into two parts and number them Supplementary Schedule No. 1 and No. 2. You can start the second schedule at location A200, as we did in our example. You may have as many sup-

```
WORKSHEET 9.2AB:   SUPPLEMENTARY SCHEDULES


      MARGINS:   LEFT=3, RIGHT=85

      COLUMNS:   GLOBAL=12

      FORMAT:    COMMAS, NO DECIMALS

      PRINTER:   COMPRESS=OFF, RANGE NAMES=SUP1 AND SUP2

      RUN:       SEMI-ANNUALLY
```

```
WORKSHEET  9.2A:   SUPPLEMENTARY SCHEDULES
------------------------------------------------------------------------------
      SUPPLEMENTARY SCHEDULES NO. 1 ... AS OF ...   22-Oct-84

      JAMES T. SOMEBODY                500 ALL-AMERICAN WAY
      JUDY R. SOMEBODY                 ANYTOWN, USA 94123
                                       (465) 987-4321

==============================================================================
         SCHEDULE A:   CASH AND BANK ACCOUNTS
------------------------------------------------------------------------------
BANK NAME            LOCATION            HELD BY     ACCT NO.      AMOUNT
------------------------------------------------------------------------------
National Bank       Anytown, USA        James       198748-67        250
Stagecoach Bank     Anytown, USA        Joint        67398-21        500
Country Bank        Anytown, USA        Judy        20987-667        250
First S&L Assoc     Anytown, Usa        Joint       1-15257-03     5,000
CrUn MoneyMktFnd    Anytown, USA        Joint          557632       2000
                                                                 -------
                                        TOTAL CASH ON HAND =     $8,000

==============================================================================
         SCHEDULE B:   STOCKS, BONDS AND OTHER SECURITIES
------------------------------------------------------------------------------
DESCRIPTION          DATE       HELD BY     #SHRS        COST   MKT VALUE
------------------------------------------------------------------------------
US Gov't Securties   18-Feb-82  Joint        100        5,000       3,000
Nxxon                24-May-83  Joint        100        3,500       4,000
Global Oil           27-Aug-84  Joint        100        1,000       2,500
                                                                -------
                                        TOTAL MARKET VALUE =      $9,500

==============================================================================
         SCHEDULE C:   IRA AND KEOGH ACCOUNTS
------------------------------------------------------------------------------
DESCRIPTION          DATE       HELD BY     UNITS        COST   MKT VALUE
------------------------------------------------------------------------------
Drey's Group         02-Jun-83  Joint        200        2,000       3,000
Bank CD's            04-Jan-84  Joint         10        2,000       2,500
                                                                -------
                                        TOTAL MARKET VALUE =      $5,500
```

58

```
WORKSHEET  9.2B:    SUPPLEMENTARY SCHEDULES
----------------------------------------------------------------------------
              SUPPLEMENTARY SCHEDULES NO. 2 ... AS OF ...  22-Oct-84

         JAMES T. SOMEBODY                500 ALL-AMERICAN WAY
         JUDY R. SOMEBODY                 ANYTOWN, USA 94123
                                          (456) 987-4321

============================================================================
           SCHEDULE D:   REAL ESTATE
----------------------------------------------------------------------------
DESCRIPTION              DATE      HELD BY       COST    MORTGAGE   MKT VALUE
----------------------------------------------------------------------------
Residence                08-May-76  Joint       50,000    30,000     110,000
Vacation cabin           03-Feb-79  Joint       25,000    21,000      35,000
                                               --------  --------    --------
                         TOTAL =   $75,000   $51,000    $145,000

============================================================================
           SCHEDULE E:   LIFE INSURANCE
----------------------------------------------------------------------------
INSURED              POLICY      BENEFICARY  INSURANCE CO      FACE AMOUNT
----------------------------------------------------------------------------
James Sombody        Term        Wife        Trudential          150,000
Judy Somebody        Term        Husband     Conn Corp.           50,000
                                                               --------
                                                              $200,000

============================================================================
           SCHEDULE F:   FINANCIAL CREDIT INFORMATION
----------------------------------------------------------------------------
NAME OF INSTITUTION      DATE      PURPOSE        ORIG AMOUNT    BALANCE
----------------------------------------------------------------------------
Credit Union             21-Mar-84  Sailboat          5,500       5,000
Country Bank             09-Jun-82  Honda '82          9,000       5,000
                                                                 -------
                                                    TOTAL =     $10,000
```

plementary schedules as you want. For example, you may construct one for yourself, one for your spouse, one for each member of your family, and a consolidated worksheet.

One final note: assets and liabilities change continually, almost daily. You need not redo your personal financial statement every week or month. But as your major assets change, it will be important to rerun your financial statement. You also should review it at least twice a year to make sure you are moving toward your financial goals.

Family Budgets

A budget is a roadmap. It tells you where you are, where you want to be, and how to get there. With the help of a personal computer, putting together a budget can be an accurate, orderly, and enlightening process.

HOW TO SET UP A SUCCESSFUL BUDGET

There are no fixed rules that apply to everyone when it comes to budgeting. The first step is to set down a specific budget. It might be easier to start with your annual figures first and then have your spreadsheet divide by 12 to get monthly expenses. Make your budget as detailed as you want; however, it should fit on one page.

When you key in your expenses, it makes it easier if, at the bottom of your spreadsheet, you

```
WORKSHEET 10.1:   PERSONAL BUDGET

MARGINS:   LEFT=5, RIGHT=75

COLUMNS:   GLOBAL=15, A=25

FORMAT:    COMMAS, NO DECIMALS

SORT BY:   MONTHLY EXPENSE, DECENDING

PRINTER:   COMPRESS=OFF

RUN AT:    YEAR END
```

WORKSHEET 10.1:   PERSONAL BUDGET

INCOME	MONTHLY	ANNUAL	PERCENT
SALARY: JAMES	2,333	28,000	58.70%
BUS INCOME: JUDY	1,250	15,000	31.45%
BONUS: JAMES	250	3,000	6.29%
TAX REFUND	83	1,000	2.10%
DIVIDENDS	33	400	0.84%
INTEREST	25	300	0.63%
TOTAL INCOME =	$3,975	$47,700	100.00%

EXPENSES	MONTHLY	ANNUAL	PERCENT
INCOME TAXES W/H	650	7,800	16.35%
MORTGAGE	540	6,480	13.58%
FOOD	450	5,400	11.32%
CABIN MORTGAGE	350	4,200	8.81%
CAR LOANS	300	3,600	7.55%
ESTIMATED TAXES	250	3,000	6.29%
SAVINGS	200	2,400	5.03%
UTILITIES/PHONE	175	2,100	4.40%
VACATIONS	150	1,800	3.77%
STOCK PURCHASE	150	1,800	3.77%
BANK CARDS	125	1,500	3.14%
INSURANCE	100	1,200	2.52%
MAINT/REPAIR	90	1,080	2.26%
PROPERTY TAX	85	1,020	2.14%
BOAT LOAN	75	900	1.89%
CONTRIBUTIONS	75	900	1.89%
CLOTHING	65	780	1.64%
TRANSPORTATION	50	600	1.26%
MED/DENTAL	35	420	0.88%
RECREATION	25	300	0.63%
PUBLICATIONS	25	300	0.63%
MISCELLANEOUS	10	120	0.25%
TOTAL EXPENSES =	$3,975	$47,700	100.00%

create a horizontal window which shows the total expenses. This allows you to distribute your expenses to different items in the budget, all the while keeping an eye on the tools at the bottom so that you don't go over your total income figure.

I recommend that you sort your budget by income and expense amount, in descending sequence. It also helps to calculate what percentage of your total budget each expenditure represents. This is accomplished by dividing each item in the budget by either the absolute total income or the absolute total expense, and copying this formula down on your spreadsheet.

For example, James Somebody's salary divided by the total income ($28,000/$47,000); (C9/$C$16). The "$" in front of the cell address is Lotus 1-2-3's notation for absolute cell addressing. This means the address can't be changed as the formula is copied to other cells.

Worksheet 10.1 shows an example of Mr. and Mrs. Somebody's income and expenses for the past year, sorted by percentage of income and expense. You may want to make some changes, such as having a separate category for savings and in-vestments. Some categories may not pertain to you at all. Estimated taxes, for example, should be included only if you usually pay more in taxes than is withheld from your paycheck. Then this category will help you plan for the excess amount.

GETTING THE MOST OUT OF YOUR PAYCHECK

Most of us never see the money we pay to the government in federal, state and local taxes. It's simply deducted from our paychecks. Sometimes the annual withholding sum will cover our total tax obligation. If we have insufficient withholding, we owe money; if we overpaid we have a refund coming. Some people prefer to overpay. In a sense, this is a form of enforced savings, except that you don't get any interest on your tax refund.

If you are self-employed, like Mrs. Somebody, you will have to make quarterly payments based on your estimated income tax due, as well as your self-employment tax (the parallel to Social Security for the employed). Because these estimated taxes are payable only four times each year, it might be tempting to forget them until they fall due. Don't,

because it might be difficult to come up with one-fourth of your annual tax bill if you have not set aside the money for those payments. One method would be to set aside the necessary amount each month so you don't have to throw your budget out of joint each quarter.

Another danger is to overestimate other forms of enforced savings like Social Security, profit sharing plans and savings deductions. These savings represent a substantial part of the resources for meeting long-range goals, particularly retirement. Many people find that their reliance on these sources has been overestimated, and there simply isn't as much as one expects. Therefore, it is vital that you monitor on a continuing basis exactly how much is deducted each year and what is available for an emergency, an opportunity, or retirement.

Worksheet 10.2 will help you analyze these aspects of your paycheck. The report shows Mr. and Mrs. Somebody's monthly and annual income, all tax deductions, business expenses and savings. It also calculates the percent of each category in the report.

PERSONAL FINANCIAL PROFILE

Worksheet 10.3 borrows income and expense information from the Personal Budget Worksheet and asset and liability data from the Personal Finan-cial Statement and combines them into one neat report.

The beauty of this worksheet is that it forces you to compress everything you earn, spend, own and owe into a one-page report. In order to do this, you may have to combine your expenditures into general categories such as personal, transportation, entertainment, shelter, etc. The worksheet also calculates the percent of each item in the report.

Worksheet 10.3 shows that the Somebodys have budgeted their income to cover all expenses except for the remote possibility of Jim Somebody losing his job, or a decline in Judy's home business. However, they seem to have sufficient assets to cover the family's needs in the event that they suffer a temporary loss of income.

FORECASTING WITH THE PC

There are two formulas which are used throughout the book for making projections and forecasts. The first illustrates the principle of *compound growth rate,* the second will compute the future value of an *annuity.*

Compounding occurs when investment income, whether interest, dividend or capital gains, is reinvested with the principal. For example, if you were to receive the interest from a savings account by check each quarter and not invest it, you would

---

```
WORKSHEET  10.2:   ANALYSIS OF PERSONAL INCOME


    MARGINS:    LEFT=5, RIGHT=75

    COLUMNS:    GLOBAL=10, A=27

    FORMAT:     COMMAS, NO DECIMALS

    PRINTER:    COMPRESS=OFF

    SORT BY:    ANNUAL AMOUNT, DESCENDING

    RUN:        MONTHLY OR ANNUALLY
```

WORKSHEET 10.2:   ANALYSIS OF PERSONAL INCOME

JAMES SOMBODY'S INCOME	ANNUAL	MONTHLY	PERCENT
SMC CORP. - SALARY	$27,000	$2,250	87.10%
- BONUS	$2,500	$208	8.06%
- AUTO ALLOWANCE	$1,500	$125	4.84%
	$31,000	$2,583	100.00%

JAMES' PAYROLL DEDUCTIONS	ANNUAL	MONTHLY	PERCENT
FEDERAL W/H TAX	$2,800	$233	9.03%
STATE W/H TAX	$671	$56	2.16%
F.I.C.A. W/H	$1,844	$154	5.95%
SMC STOCK PLAN - 10%	$2,800	$233	9.03%
CREDIT UNION - 5%	$1,350	$113	4.35%
UNITED WAY - 2%	$600	$50	1.94%
TAX DEFERRED SAVINGS PLAN	$1,000	$83	3.23%
IRA ACCOUNT	$2,000	$167	6.45%
TOTAL =	$13,065	$1,089	42.15%
JAMES' NET PAY =	$17,935	$1,495	57.85%

JUDY SOMEBODY'S INCOME	ANNUAL	MONTHLY	PERCENT
GROSS BUSINESS INCOME	$25,000	$2,083	100.00%
COST OF GOODS SOLD	$4,000	$333	16.00%
BUSINESS EXPENSES	$5,000	$417	20.00%
DEPRECIATION	$1,000	$83	4.00%
BEFORE TAX NET INCOME =	$15,000	$1,250	60.00%
FERERAL TAXES	$1,672	$139	6.69%
STATE TAXES	$334	$28	1.34%
F.I.C.A	$974	$81	3.90%
TOTAL =	$2,980	$248	11.92%
AFTER TAX NET INCOME =	$12,020	$1,002	48.08%
KEOGH ACCOUNT	$1,500	$125	6.00%
JUDY'S NET PAY =	$10,520	$877	42.08%

receive simple interest, not compound interest. If you were to leave the interest on deposit and get interest on interest, you would have compound interest.

Over long periods of time, the amount of money that can be earned by compounding is significant. For example, how much will an investment of $100,000 be worth in twenty years if it grows at an annual compounded growth rate of 12 percent. The answer is $964,629 if we compound annually, and $1,089,255 if we compound monthly. This amount is more than three times the $360,000 that you would have achieved through a simple return.

The second formula will compute the future value of an annuity. An annuity is a series of equal payments made at regular intervals of time. The time intervals between payments are called payment periods. The difference between this and the previous formula is that an annuity is a compound interest situation with periodic payments. For example, how much will your IRA be worth if you contribute $2,000 per year for the next 15 years and it earns 8 percent interest? Using the 1-2-3 formula for future value, the answer is $54,304.

These formulas are very useful for forecasting and asking "What if" type questions. The formula for compounding an asset is straightforward and easy to program with 1-2-3, and is illustrated below and in Worksheet 10.4. The arithmetic operator which indicates exponentiation is shown as the ^ character.

$$\text{Value of the Asset} = \text{Present Value} \times (1 + \text{Rate of Return}) \wedge \text{Payment Period}$$

The formula for computing the future value of an annuity uses a built-in Lotus 1-2-3 function called @FV:

@FV = (Payment Amount, Growth Rate, Payment Periods)

PROJECTION OF EXPENSES

After you have constructed your personal budget as outlined earlier, divide your budget items into two parts: (1) the inflation-resistant items that remain constant over the years, and (2) the items that vary with inflation.

Next we want to construct a spreadsheet like the example illustrated in Worksheet 10.5. In that worksheet, you will project what you think the annual rate of inflation will be for the next five years and have the computer calculate what effect inflation will have on your variable expenses.

Use the annual expense figures from your personal budget worksheet. I suggest that you work with only those expenses over $1,000 and group the rest. Pay close attention to future costs, e.g., education or transportation—especially if you have children who will be in college and want their own cars. If tuition upsets your budget, indicate how much borrowing you'll have to do to pay those future expenses.

```
WORKSHEET  10.3:   PERSONAL FINANCIAL PROFILE

MARGINS:   LEFT=5, RIGHT=75

COLUMNS:   GLOBAL=10, A=25, B=18

FORMAT:    COMMAS, NO DECIMALS

PRINTER:   COMPRESS=OFF

SORT BY:   AMOUNT WITHIN EACH CATEGORY, DESCENDING

RUN:       QUARTERLY
```

PROFILE   22-Oct-84

WORKSHEET 10.3: PERSONAL FINANCIAL PROFILE

INCOME	ANNUAL	PERCENT
===========================	==========	==========
JAMES: SALARY/BONUS	31,000	64.99%
BUS INCOME: JUDY	15,000	31.45%
TAX REFUND	1,000	2.10%
Interest/Dividend	700	1.47%
TOTAL INCOME =	$47,700	100.00%

EXPENSES	ANNUAL	PERCENT
===========================	==========	==========
MORTGAGES & PROP TAXES	11,700	24.53%
TAXES: FIT/FICA/STATE	10,800	22.64%
FOOD & CHILDREN'S EXPENSES	5,400	11.32%
LOANS: AUTOS/BOAT	4,500	9.43%
SAVINGS/INVESTMENTS	4,200	8.81%
UTILITIES/PHONE	2,100	4.40%
ENTERTAIN/VACATIONS	1,800	3.77%
BANK CARDS/INTEREST	1,500	3.14%
INSURANCE: HOME/AUTO/LIFE	1,200	2.52%
HOME MAINT/REPAIRS	1,080	2.26%
CONTRIBUTIONS/CHARITY	900	1.89%
CLOTHING/MISC	900	1.89%
TRANSPORTATION	600	1.26%
EDUCATION/PUBLICATIONS	600	1.26%
MEDICAL/DENTAL	420	0.88%
TOTAL EXPENSES =	$47,700	100.00%

ASSETS	AMOUNT	PERCENT
===========================	==========	==========
RESIDENCE	110,000	54.59%
VACATION CABIN	35,000	17.37%
PERSONAL PROPERTY	16,000	7.94%
AUTOMOBILES	12,000	5.96%
SAILBOAT	5,500	2.73%
STOCKS & SECURITIES	9,500	4.71%
SAVINGS & CHECKING ACCTS	8,000	3.97%
IRA & KEOGH	5,500	2.73%
TOTAL ASSETS =	$201,500	100.00%

LIABILITIES	AMOUNT	PERCENT
===========================	==========	==========
MORTAGES	51,000	77.33%
LOANS: AUTO/BOAT	10,000	15.16%
CURRENT BILLS	4,950	7.51%
TOTAL LIABILITIES =	$65,950	100.00%

NET WORTH = $135,550

66

```
       WORKSHEET  10.4:  TWO FORECASTING FORMULAS


       MARGINS:  LEFT=5, RIGTH=75

       COLUMNS:  A=31, B=12, C=2, D=20

       FORMAT:   COMMAS, NO DECIMALS

       PRINTER:  COMPRESS=OFF

       RUN:      AS NEEDED
```

```
WHATIF                                              22-Oct-84

WORKSHEET  10.4:  TWO FORECASTING FORMULAS

------------------------------------------------------------
VARIABLES                    CALCULATION   LOTUS FORMULAS
============================================================

COMPOUND GROWTH RATE
================================

A.  PRESENT VALUE              $100,000

B.  ANNUAL RATE OF GROWTH        12.00%

C.  NUMBER OF YEARS                  20

D.  VALUE OF IN "C" YEARS      $964,629    A*(1+B)^C



FUTURE VALUE OF AN ANNUITY
================================

E.  SAVINGS PER YEAR             $2,000

F.  ANNUAL RATE OF RETURN         8.00%

G.  PAYMENT PERIOD                   15

H.  FUTURE VALUE OF SAVINGS     $54,304    @FV(E,F,G)
```

For example, instead of budgeting $8,000 in one year for college education, assume that you will get a loan and that you'll pay it back at the rate of $2,000 per year for the next five years.

Remember that some of these factors are estimates and projections and do not require precise data. Once you've set up the worksheet you can change the inflation rate to 4 percent or 8 percent

```
        WORKSHEET 10.5:   BUDGET PLANNING WORKSHEET

        MARGINS:   LEFT=5, RIGHT=85

        COLUMNS:   GLOBAL=15, A=25

        FORMAT:    COMMAS, NO DECIMALS

        PRINTER:   COMPRESS=OFF

        RUN AT:    YEAR END
```

BUDPLAN   22-Oct-84

WORKSHEET 10.5:   BUDGET PLANNING WORKSHEET

```
-----------------------------------------------------------------
EXPENDITURES          CURRENT     FIVE YEARS      TEN YEARS
=================================================================

INFLATION RESISTANT
------------------------
HOUSE MORTGAGE          6,480        6,480          6,480
CAR LOANS               3,600            0          4,000
INSURANCE               1,200        1,300          1,200
CABIN MORTGAGE          4,200        4,200          4,200
PROPERTY TAX            1,020        1,020          1,020
BOAT LOAN                 900            0              0
                      --------     --------        --------
        TOTAL =       $17,400      $13,000        $16,900



INFLATION AT:
            6.00%      CURRENT      5 YEARS        10 YEARS
-----------------------------------------------------------------
UTILITIES/PHONE         3,200        4,282          5,731
MAINT/REPAIRS           1,080        1,445          1,934
FOOD                    7,400        9,903         13,252
TRANSPORTATION            800        1,071          1,433
TAXES                  10,800       14,453         19,341
MISCELLANEOUS           5,000        6,691          8,954
VACATIONS               1,800        2,409          3,224
                      --------     --------        --------
        TOTAL =       $30,080      $40,254        $53,869

  GRAND TOTAL =       $47,480      $53,254        $70,769
                      ========     ========        ========
```

ANALYSIS OF A BUDGET

An analysis of your budget can reveal some interesting things. Start with your yearly estimate of income and expenses computed in Worksheet 10.1.

Group your expenditures and their amounts according to the general categories illustrated in Worksheet 10.3 An easy way to do this is to enter the total expenditure amount at the bottom of the column, and have it equal the sum of the expenditures above it. Then, as you key in each expenditure, you can watch the total at the bottom of your screen.

Next, enter the normal range of distribution of budgeted funds, as provided by the United States Census Bureau, and have the worksheet calculate your percent distribution of budgeted expenses. Remember to divide each of your expenditures by the absolute total expenses figure. Then copy this formula down your column for the rest of the expenditures.

It is important to analyze this information in order to decide if you are satisfied with the distribution of your expenses. For example, as your income increases, the percentage you spend on taxes will increase. You may decide, after studying Worksheet 10.6, that more of your savings should go to tax sheltered or tax-free investments.

Worksheet 10.6 shows Mr. and Mrs. Somebody's distribution of budgeted funds compared to the normal distribution of budgeted funds.

BALANCING YOUR CHECKBOOK

This next worksheet is a simple application of Lotus 1-2-3, but one that might be useful for tracking and balancing several bank accounts, or the account of a friend or elderly relative.

If you have multiple checking accounts like a business account, a personal account, your spouse's account, etc., you can use this worksheet as a bill-paying account. You can keep most of your money in an interest-bearing account for as long as possible, and then move funds into this bill-paying account when the bills are due. To construct this model, enter the information as shown in the sample worksheet 10.7A. Then enter the check

or whatever you want and see what effect it will have on your future budget.

Worksheet 10.5 is a projection for Mr. and Mrs. Somebody's expenses for the next five years, with the inflation rate running at 6 percent per year. If you use absolute values for the expense amount and the rate of inflation, you can vary these and see what effect it has on expenditures in five or 10 years. The formula for calculating the future value of an expense is shown below using the following variables:

Expense = \$6,480, Inflation = 6 percent, Number of years $= {}^\wedge 5$:

$(6,480) * (1.06)^\wedge 5$

number, the date, a brief description, and the amount of each deposit and/or withdrawal in the appropriate columns. The worksheet will compute the running balance using the following formula:

IF(D8, = 0#AND#E8< = 0,@ err, + F6 – D8 + – E8)

The @**IF** function is used to check the cells that may contain a check withdrawal or deposit, to see if they really do. Thus if both cells are empty, the ERR value is stored in the running balance field.

Otherwise, the running balance is updated by adding the deposit and subtracting the payment.

DISTRIBUTING YOUR EXPENSES

Worksheet 10.7A easily can be changed so that it will allow you to distribute and accumulate your expenses as you enter them into your checkbook. Transportation expenses, for example, could be account code 5. When you make your checkbook entry for transportation, you enter it with the code 5 and the worksheet automatically will post it to

---

```
WORKSHEET 10.6:  DISTRIBUTION OF BUDGETED FUNDS

MARGINS:   RIGHT=5, LEFT= 75

COLUMNS:   GLOBAL=15, A=20

FORMAT:    COMMAS, NO DECIMALS

SORT BY:   NORMAL PERCENTAGE

PRINTER:   COMPRESS=OFF

RUN AT:    YEAR END
```

BUDDISTR   22-Oct-84

WORKSHEET 10.6:   DISTRIBUTION OF BUDGETED FUNDS

EXPENDITURES	NORMAL PERCENT	SOMEBODYS' AMOUNT	SOMEBODYS' PERCENT
HOUSING	25.00%	12,780	26.79%
FOOD	23.00%	5,400	11.32%
FED/STATE TAXES	13.00%	7,000	14.68%
PERSONAL	10.00%	9,900	20.75%
TRANSPORTATION	8.00%	1,000	2.10%
OTHER	7.00%	5,000	10.48%
SOCIAL SECURITY	5.00%	3,800	7.97%
SAVINGS	5.00%	2,400	5.03%
MEDICAL/DENTAL	4.00%	420	0.88%
	100.00%	$47,700	100.00%

the correct account. It is very easy to do—you simply use 1-2-3's @IF statement.

The first thing to do is make a copy of Worksheet 10.7A and add a final total for payments and deposits. We arbitrarily set our total line at Row 40. If you need more rows you simply expand the range of the worksheet.

You also will need to add a column for the checkbook code, and the descriptions of our ex-pense codes at the top of the worksheet. When you make your checkbook entry, the worksheet will compare the check code to a numeric expense code which starts in column AA12 and continues through column AL12. If the checkbook code matches an expense code, the payment amount is automatically distributed to the appropriate column. The formula for distributing the check amount should be entered in every cell starting at column AA16 through

---

WORKSHEET 10.7A: BALANCING YOUR CHECKBOOK

MARGINS: LEFT=5, RIGHT=85

COLUMNS: GLOBAL=10, A=7, B=8, C=25

PRINTER: COMPRESS=OFF

RUN: AS NEEDED

CHECKS   22-Oct-84

WORKSHEET 10.7A: BALANCE CHECKBOOK

CHECK #	DATE	DESCRIPTION	PAYMENT	DEPOSIT	BALANCE
		TOTALS =	$1,606.29	$750.00	$540.34
101	25-Jan	Bud's Service Station	50.00		490.34
102	25-Jan	Mutual Family Insurance	175.00		315.34
	25-Jan	Transfer from savings		500.00	815.34
103	26-Jan	Realty Mortgage Co	450.00		365.34
104	27-Jan	Cash	50.00		315.34
105	02-Feb	Dr. Robinson DDS	75.00		240.34
	05-Feb	Gasco dividend check		250.00	490.34
106	05-Feb	Public Light Co.	55.13		435.21
107	10-Feb	Modern Times Magazine	29.95		405.26
108	10-Feb	Credit Card Corp.	350.78		54.48
109	12-Feb	Telephone Co	27.55		26.93
110	15-Feb	XYZ stock purchase	250.00		(223.07)
111	16-Feb	Cash	50.00		(273.07)
112	18-Feb	Family Market	42.88		(315.95)
					ERR
					ERR
					ERR
					ERR
					ERR

WORKSHEET 10.7B&C: BALANCE CHECKBOOK & DISTRIBUTE EXPENSES

MARGINS: LEFT=0, RIGHT=136

COLUMNS: GLOBAL=10, A=7, B=8, E=4, G=22

PRINTER: COMPRESS=OFF FOR CHECKBOOK, ON FOR DISTRIBUTION

RANGES: CHECKBOOK=CHK, DISTRIBUTION=DIST

RUN: AS NEEDED

CHECKS   22-Oct-84

WORKSHEET 10.7B: BALANCE YOUR CHECKBOOK & DISTRIBUTE EXPENSES

CODES: 1= FOOD   5= TRANSPORTATION   9= MED/DENTAL
         2= UTILITIES   6= SAVINGS & INVESTMENT 10= PERSONAL
         3= HOUSING   7= EDUCATION/PUBS   11= CLOTHING
         4= TAXES   8= ENTERTAIN/VACATIONS 12= CONTRIBUTIONS

CHECK NO.	DATE	CODE	DESCRIPTION	PAYMENT	DEPOSIT	BALANCE
					BALANCE =	$540.34
101	25-Jan	5	Bud's Service Station	50.00		490.34
102	25-Jan	3	Mutual Home Insurance	175.00		315.34
	25-Jan		Transfer from savings		500.00	815.34
103	26-Jan	3	Realty Mortgage Co	450.00		365.34
104	27-Jan	10	Cash	50.00		315.34
105	02-Feb	9	Dr. Robinson DDS	75.00		240.34
	05-Feb		Gasco dividend check		250.00	490.34
106	05-Feb	2	Public Light Co.	55.13		435.21
107	10-Feb	7	Modern Times Magazine	29.95		405.26
108	10-Feb	10	Credit Card Corp.	350.78		54.48
109	12-Feb	2	Telephone Co	27.55		26.93
110	15-Feb	6	XYZ stock purchase	250.00		(223.07)
111	16-Feb	10	Cash	50.00		(273.07)
112	18-Feb	1	Family Market	42.88		(315.95)
						ERR
						ERR
						ERR
						ERR
						ERR
						ERR
						ERR
						ERR
						ERR
						ERR
			TOTALS =	1,606.29	750.00	

73

WORKSHEET 10.7C: BALANCE YOUR CHECKBOOK & DISTRIBUTE EXPENSES

CODES:	1= FOOD		5= TRANSPORTATION	9= MED/DENTAL
	2= UTILITIES		6= SAVINGS & INVESTMENTS	10= PERSONAL
	3= HOUSING		7= EDUCATION/PUBS	11= CLOTHING
	4= TAXES		8= ENTERTAIN/VACATIONS	12= CONTRIBUTIONS

1	2	3	4	5	6	7	8	9	10	11	12
FOOD	UTIL	HOUSING	TAXES	TRANS	SAVINGS	EDUC/PUBS	ENTERTAIN	MED/DENTAL	PERSONAL	CLOTHING	CONTRIB
0	0	0	0	50	0	0	0	0	0	0	0
0	0	175	0	0	0	0	0	0	0	0	0
0	0	0	0	0	0	0	0	0	0	0	0
0	0	450	0	0	0	0	0	0	0	0	0
0	0	0	0	0	0	0	0	0	50	0	0
0	0	0	0	0	0	0	0	75	0	0	0
0	0	0	0	0	0	0	0	0	0	0	0
0	55.13	0	0	0	0	0	0	0	0	0	0
0	0	0	0	0	0	29.95	0	0	0	0	0
0	0	0	0	0	0	0	0	0	350.78	0	0
0	27.55	0	0	0	0	0	0	0	0	0	0
0	0	0	0	0	250	0	0	0	0	0	0
0	0	0	0	0	0	0	0	0	50	0	0
42.88	0	0	0	0	0	0	0	0	0	0	0
0	0	0	0	0	0	0	0	0	0	0	0
0	0	0	0	0	0	0	0	0	0	0	0
0	0	0	0	0	0	0	0	0	0	0	0
0	0	0	0	0	0	0	0	0	0	0	0
0	0	0	0	0	0	0	0	0	0	0	0
0	0	0	0	0	0	0	0	0	0	0	0
0	0	0	0	0	0	0	0	0	0	0	0
0	0	0	0	0	0	0	0	0	0	0	0
0	0	0	0	0	0	0	0	0	0	0	0
$42.88	$82.68	$625.00	$0.00	$50.00	$250.00	$29.95	$0.00	$75.00	$450.78	$0.00	$0.00

TOTAL = $1,606.29

AL16, and continuing down through every row of the checkbook. The formula takes the following form:

@IF(Check Code = Expense Code, Check Amount, O)

Translated, this means if the check code equals the expense code, then enter the check amount in this cell. Otherwise enter a zero in this cell. You will have to use an absolute address for both the check code and the check amount. The expense code will be the same for all cells in the same column. A total of the accumulated expenses can be used to crossfoot to the checkbook payment total. This will assure you that all your checkbook payments were entered with a valid expense code.

BILLS
LOOSE ENDS
MISC
FILING
MEMOS
RUSH
NEXT
OUT
IN

YE OLE FAMILY BUSINESS

MONTHLY BUSINESS EXPENSES

Much of the value of a personal computer lies in the user's ability to set up meaningful expense budgets for various home businesses. Individuals with sole proprietorships are required to use Schedule C of the IRS 1040 Tax Form to report any business profit or loss. We can use 1-2-3 to set up a model which is the equivalent of the deductions portion of the IRS schedule. Worksheet 10.8 is an example of this model using Judy Somebody's monthly expense statement for her home decorator business.

WORKSHEET 10.8: MONTHLY BUSINESS EXPENSES

MARGINS: LEFT=0, RIGHT=136

COLUMNS: GLOBAL=10, A=15

FORMAT: NO COMMAS

PRINTER: COMPRESS=ON

RUN AT: MONTH-END

BUDEXP

WORKSHEET 10.8: MONTHLY BUSINESS EXPENSES ... AS OF ...   Oct-84   22-Oct-84

EXPENDITURES	JAN	FEB	MAR	APR	MAY	JUN	JUL	AUG	SEP	OCT	NOV	DEC	YTD TOTALS
ADVERTISING			75		75		25		75		75		325
BAD DEBTS	105												105
BANK SERV CHGS													0
CAR EXPENSES	25	25	25	25	25	25	25	25	25	25	25	25	300
DEPLETION													0
DEPRECIATION	80	80	80	80	80	80	80	80	80	80	80	80	960
FREIGHT			55				45						100
INSURANCE	150						150						300
INTEREST													0
LEGAL EXP													0
OFFICE EXP	15	15	15	15	15	15	15	15	15	15	15	15	180
REPAIRS	10	10	10	10	10	10	10	10	10	10	10	10	120
SUPPLIES													0
TAXES			700			700			700			700	2,800
TRAVEL/ENT	12	12	12	12	12	12	12	12	12	12	12	12	144
UTILITIES	10	10	10	10	10	10	10	10	10	10	10	10	120
	407	152	982	152	227	852	372	152	927	152	227	852	5,454

The worksheet expenditures are similar to those in the IRS schedule, except that only those expenses that pertain to Judy's business are included. The worksheet is constructed with 13 columns so that a cumulative total is available for tracking year-to-date expenses.

The source of the expenditures could be a business checkbook like the one illustrated in Worksheet 10.7A, and itemized expenses could be automatically distributed as described in our previous worksheets.

Cash Flow Analysis

There are many people who like to analyze their household income and expenses on a monthly basis. This is particularly true of those who are on a tight budget.

MONTHLY CASH FLOW

Now that we have constructed an annual budget and estimated the effects of inflation, we are ready to set up a worksheet that will help you track your monthly cash flow.

You can start by retrieving the Personal Financial Profile, Worksheet 10.3, and using it as the basis for your monthly cash flow. In order for the 12 months of the year to fit on one page, you will have to combine and reduce the number of income and expense categories. Worksheet 11.1 illustrates how to set up your monthly cash flow statement.

The beginning balance at the top of the

```
WORKSHEET  11.1:   MONTHLY CASH FLOW

MARGINS:   LEFT=5, RIGHT=85

COLUMNS:   GLOBAL-9, A-15

FORMAT:    COMMAS, NO DECIMALS, $'S ON TOTALS ONLY

PRINTER:   COMPRESS=OFF

RUN:       MONTHLY
```

WORKSHEET 11.1: MONTHLY CASH FLOW

===

	JAN	FEB	MAR	APR	MAY	JUN
BEGIN BAL	$0	$200	$183	$66	$24	$82
INCOME:						
JIM	2,333	2,333	2,333	2,333	2,333	2,333
JUDY	1,250	1,250	1,250	1,250	1,250	1,250
OTHER	392		200		300	
TOTAL =	$3,975	$3,783	$3,966	$3,649	$3,907	$3,665
EXPENSES:						
FOOD	450	450	375	450	450	450
SHELTER	990	990	990	990	990	990
MEDICAL	35	35	35	35	35	35
TRANSP	140	140	140	140	140	140
PERSONAL	300	500	500	400	350	350
ENTERTAIN	125	125	125	125	125	125
TAXES	1,125	750	1,125	1,125	1,125	1,125
UTIL	175	175	175	175	175	175
SAVINGS	350	350	350	100	350	100
CHARITY	85	85	85	85	85	85
TOTAL =	$3,775	$3,600	$3,900	$3,625	$3,825	$3,575
END BAL =	$200	$183	$66	$24	$82	$90

===

	JUL	AUG	SEP	OCT	NOV	DEC
BEGIN BAL	$90	$148	$281	$114	$422	$330
INCOME						
JIM	2,333	2,333	2,333	2,333	2,333	2,333
JUDY	1,250	1,250	1,250	1,250	1,250	1,250
OTHER	100	250		450	300	
TOTAL =	3,773	3,981	3,864	4,147	4,305	3,913
EXPENSES						
FOOD	450	450	375	450	450	450
SHELTER	990	990	990	990	990	990
MEDICAL	35	35	35	35	35	35
TRANSP	140	140	140	140	140	140
PERSONAL	300	400	350	250	500	400
ENTERTAIN	125	125	125	125	125	125
TAXES	1,125	1,000	1,125	1,125	1,125	1,125
UTIL	175	175	175	175	175	175
SAVINGS	200	300	350	350	350	300
CHARITY	85	85	85	85	85	85
TOTAL =	$3,625	$3,700	$3,750	$3,725	$3,975	$3,825
END BAL =	$148	$281	$114	$422	$330	$88

worksheet is added to the total monthly income. Monthly living expenses are entered for each major category and subtracted from total income to produce our monthly ending balance. This total becomes the beginning balance for the next month, and so forth through the rest of the year.

This worksheet could be used both as a forecast and as an actual history of your monthly cash flow. Each month you simply replace your estimate of the monthly income and expenses with the actual expenditures, and have the worksheet recalculate the beginning and ending monthly balances.

You also could expand this worksheet by adding a planned dollar amount for each item in the budget and comparing it to the actual amount spent. A year-to-date total could also be included for each expenditure.

A HISTORY OF YOUR CASH FLOW

Many people like to analyze their household expenses over a number of years. Again, this is particularly true of those on a tight budget. This next worksheet will assist those of you who have this need.

You will have to go back a few years and enter your income and expenses for the past five years. Don't worry if your detailed financial records don't go back five years. Just determine the income and expense totals for those prior years and enter in your expenditures as best you can remember them. A miscellaneous row can be used to make your individual expenses match your annual totals.

The easy way to build this worksheet is to have Lotus 1-2-3 retrieve Worksheet 10.1 (Personal Budget), and delete the MONTHLY column and change the headings from ANNUAL to last year's date (e.g., 1983). Then a quick way to set up the formats in the columns for the four prior years is to copy 1983's expenses across the four additional years, then delete or change the expenditures for each individual year.

For next year's analysis, you simply insert a new column in front of 1983 and you are set. This report can be very informative because it will help you spot trends like significant increases in any one category, or what the trend has been for any one item over the past five years.

Worksheet 11.2 is an example of Mr. and Mrs. Somebody's income and expenses for the past five years. Notice that even though all the information is not filled in, the Somebodys could still make reasonable predictions regarding next year's bonus and tax refund.

SOURCES AND USES OF FUNDS

Worksheet 11.3 is an excellent and necessary money management tool. The Source and Allocation of Funds report is set up at the beginning of

---

WORKSHEET 11.2:   HISTORY OF ANNUAL CASH FLOW

MARGINS: LEFT=5, RIGHT=85

COLUMNS: GLOBAL=10, A=20

FORMAT: COMMAS, NO DECIMALS, $ ON TOTALS ONLY

SORT BY: EXPENDITURE AMOUNT, DECENDING SEQUENCE

PRINTER: COMPRESS=OFF

RUN AT: YEAR END

WORKSHEET 11.2:   HISTORY OF ANNUAL CASH FLOW

INCOME	1983	1982	1981	1980	1979
SALARY: JAMES	28,000	27,000	26,000	25,000	20,000
NET INCOME: JUDY	15,000	12,000	9,000	2,000	0
BONUS: JAMES	3,000	2,500	1,200	500	200
TAX REFUND	1,000	400	300	100	200
DIVIDENDS	400	350	250	150	75
INTEREST	300	250	225	200	175
TOTAL INCOME =	$47,700	$42,500	$36,975	$27,950	$20,650

EXPENSES	1983	1982	1981	1980	1979
TAXES	10,800	10,120	9,165	6,500	4,600
MORTGAGE	6,480	6,480	6,360	6,100	4,500
FOOD	5,400	5,100	4,800	4,600	4,000
CABIN MORTGAGE	4,200	4,000	3,800	3,500	3,200
CAR LOANS	3,600	3,500	3,400	2,500	
SAVINGS	2,400	2,200	1,500		
UTILITIES/PHONE	2,100	2,000			
STOCK PURCHASE	1,800	1,000	800		
VACATIONS	1,800	1,500			
BANK CARDS	1,500	1,200	900		
INSURANCE	1,200	1,100	1,000	1,050	900
MAINT/REPAIR	1,080	1,000			
PROPERTY TAX	1,020	1,000	950	900	850
CONTRIBUTIONS	900				
BOAT LOAN	900				
CLOTHING	780				
TRANSPORTATION	600				
MED/DENTAL	420				
RECREATION	300				
PUBLICATIONS	300				
MISCELLANEOUS	120	2,300	4,300	2,800	2,600
TOTAL EXPENSES =	$47,700	$42,500	$36,975	$27,950	$20,650

the year. It estimates the date, the source and the amount of money you expect to receive for investment purposes over the next 12 months, and then helps you to allocate these funds according to your investment goals.

For example, income might come from moonlighting, a tax refund, bonuses, interest from savings, dividends, or the sale of some stock or other investment. The worksheet allows you to plan where, when, and how these funds will be invested or used (you could spend your windfall on a vacation). When you actually receive the money, you record the date and actual amount received and where it was invested or used.

This worksheet will have an immediate effect on improving the rate of return on your investments and will show you how to take on larger investments and pay for them with smaller sources

```
        WORKSHEET  11.3:  SOURCE AND ALLOCATION OF FUNDS
        MARGINS:   RIGHT=3, RIGHT =85
        COLUMNS:   GLOBAL =12
        FORMAT:    COMMAS, NO DECIMALS
        PRINTER:   COMPRESS=OFF
        SORT BY:   ESTIMATED DATE
        RUN AT:    BEGINNING OF YEAR AND AS NEEDED
```

```
ALLOCATE                                              22-Oct-84

WORKSHEET  11.3:  SOURCE AND ALLOCATION OF INVESTMENT FUNDS
-----------------------------------------------------------------

-----------ESTIMATED-------------- ||----------------ACTUAL--------------
  DATE  :   SOURCE     :  AMOUNT  ||   DATE    : ALLOCATION  :  AMOUNT
======== :============ :========== ||========== :============ :==========
 Jan-84 :JIM'S SALARY :     $150  || 15-Jan-84 :CREDIT UNION :   $150.00
 Jan-84 :JIM'S BONUS  :     $500  || 10-Jan-84 :DREY'S FUND  :   $450.75
        :             :           ||           :             :
 Feb-84 :JIM'S SALARY :     $150  || 15-Feb-84 :CREDIT UNION :   $150.00
        :             :           ||           :             :
 Mar-84 :JIM'S SALARY :     $150  || 15-Mar-84 :CREDIT UNION :   $150.00
 Mar-84 :INTEREST     :      $75  || 15-Mar-84 :SAVINGS ACCT :    $75.25
 Mar-84 :SMC DIVIDEND :      $50  || 15-Mar-84 :SMC CORP     :    $50.15
        :             :           ||           :             :
 Apr-84 :JIM'S SALARY :     $150  || 15-Apr-84 :CREDIT UNION :   $150.00
 Apr-84 :STOCK SALE   :   $1,000  || 16-Apr-84 :DREY'S FUND  : $1,104.34
        :             :           ||           :             :
 May-84 :JIM'S SALARY :     $150  || 15-May-84 :CREDIT UNION :   $150.00
 May-84 :JIM'S BONUS  :     $500  || 18-May-84 :DREY'S FUND  :   $450.00
        :             :           ||           :             :
 Jun-84 :JIM'S SALARY :     $150  || 15-Jun-84 :CREDIT UNION :   $150.00
 Jun-84 :INTEREST     :      $75  || 15-Jun-84 :SAVINGS ACCT :    $85.38
 Jun-84 :SMC DIVIDEND :      $60  || 15-Jun-84 :SMC CORP     :    $65.55
        :             :           ||           :             :
 Jul-84 :JIM'S SALARY :     $150  || 15-Jul-84 :CREDIT UNION :   $150.00
 Jul-84 :JUDY'S BUS   :   $1,500  || 15-Jul-84 :STAR FUND    : $1,700.00
        :             :           ||           :             :
 Aug-84 :JIM'S SALARY :     $150  || 15-Aug-84 :CREDIT UNION :   $150.00
        :             :           ||           :             :
 Sep-84 :JIM'S SALARY :     $150  || 15-Sep-84 :CREDIT UNION :
 Sep-84 :INTEREST     :      $75  || 15-Sep-84 :SAVINGS ACCT :
 Sep-84 :SMC DIVIDEND :      $70  || 15-Sep-84 :SMC CORP     :
 Sep-84 :STOCK SALE   :   $1,000  || 16-Sep-84 :DREY'S FUND  :
        :             :           ||           :             :
 Oct-84 :JIM'S SALARY :     $150  || 15-Oct-84 :CREDIT UNION :
 Oct-84 :JIM'S BONUS  :     $500  || 18-Oct-84 :DREY'S FUND  :
        :             :           ||           :             :
 Nov-84 :JIM'S SALARY :     $150  || 15-Nov-84 :CREDIT UNION :
 Nov-84 :STOCK SALE   :   $1,000  || 16-Nov-84 :DREY'S FUND  :
        :             :           ||           :             :
 Dec-84 :JIM'S SALARY :     $150  || 15-Dec-84 :CREDIT UNION :
 Dec-84 :INTEREST     :      $75  || 18-Dec-84 :SAVINGS ACCT :
 Dec-84 :SMC DIVIDEND :      $75  || 18-Dec-84 :SAVINGS ACCT :
---------:-------------:---------- ||-----------:-------------:----------
         TOTAL =         $8,355   ||              TOTAL =      $5,181.42
                     ============                          ============
```

of income. For example, if you receive four dividend checks per year you may be tempted to spend them rather than reinvest them. This would be a mistake because reinvested dividends add to the compounding effect of your investment. Dividend checks have a way of adding up to larger sums (see Worksheet 17.5), especially when combined with other small but regular savings.

At year end you will have a complete picture of where and how you invested your discretionary funds. You can use this information to plan next year. You also can use it to see what your return was for the funds invested during the prior year.

Worksheet 11.3 shows that Mr. Somebody regularly saves $150 a month from his paycheck and banks it in his credit union. Any bonuses or other income from Judy's business goes into two mutual funds. Not shown is the monthly amount taken out to purchased SMC stock.

SECTION 5

PLANNING

Asset Management and Analysis

Upon completion of your personal financial state-ment and budget worksheets, the next step is a detailed analysis of your investment portfolio. This analysis contains six easy-to-read worksheets, which are described in this chapter.

PRESENT LIST OF INVESTMENTS
The first worksheet shows your present list of assets, classified according to type of security and industry. A sample of Mr. Somebody's present in-vestments appears in Worksheet 12.1.

```
WORKSHEET   12.1:   PRESENT LIST OF INVESTMENTS


MARGINS:    LEFT=3, RIGHT=5

COLUMNS:    GLOBAL=10, A=15

FORMAT:     COMMAS, NO DECIMALS

PRINTER:    COMPRESS=OFF

RUN:        AS NEEDED
```

WORKSHEET 12.1:   PRESENT LIST OF INVESTMENTS

INVESTMENT	COST	TOTAL RETURN	INCOME	RECENT MKT VALUE	PERCENT OF FUND
SAVINGS	8,000	5.25%	420	8,000	13.79%
NXXON CORP	3,500	9.00%	360	4,000	6.90%
GLOBIL OIL	1,000	9.00%	225	2,500	4.31%
GOV'T BONDS	5,000	7.50%	225	3,000	5.17%
VACATION CABIN	25,000	5.00%	1,750	35,000	60.34%
DREY'S FUND	2,000	12.00%	360	3,000	5.17%
BANK CD'S	2,000	12.00%	300	2,500	4.31%
	$46,500		$3,640	$58,000	100.00%

The worksheet includes the original cost figures, estimates of this year's gross annual income, and the recent market values of each for the securities in your portfolio. Additionally, the worksheet should calculate the percentage that each investment represents in your portfolio.

A HISTORY OF INVESTMENT INCOME

Worksheet 12.2 is an optional report, which could be integrated with and made part of the previous worksheet. It shows the history of income derived from all investment over the past five years. This income is shown on a cumulative basis for each investment as well as overall investments.

RETURN ON ASSETS

The next analysis of assets is important when you are deciding what to do with your discretionary

WORKSHEET 12.2:   HISTORY OF INVESTMENT INCOME

MARGINS: LEFT=5, RIGHT=85

COLUMNS: GLOBAL=10, A=15

FORMAT: COMMAS, NO DECIMALS

PRINTER: COMPRESS=OFF

RUN: AS NEEDED

WORKSHEET 12.2:   HISTORY OF INVESTMENT INCOME

	1979	1980	1981	1982	1983	CUMMULATIVE
SAVINGS	$100	$200	$250	$300	$420	$1,270
STOCKS	$23	$67	$125	$432	$585	$1,232
GOV'T BONDS	$55	$175	$225	$300	$225	$980
REAL ESTATE	$250	$750	$900	$1,250	$1,750	$4,900
IRA	$0	$0	$0	$0	$660	$660
	$428	$1,192	$1,500	$2,282	$3,640	$9,042
CUMULATIVE TO	$428	$1,620	$3,120	$5,402	$9,042	

THE MONEY MACHINE

cash in the upcoming year.

Worksheet 12.3A shows Mr. Somebody's current working assets, the estimated return on investment, and what percentage it represents of his total return. The weighted average return on investment is calculated for each asset by multiplying the estimated return by the percentage of total return (e.g., 5.25 percent × 13.55 percent = .071 percent).

An analysis of our example shows that Mr. Somebody is projecting an average rate of return of 8.61 percent on assets of $58,000. If we shift his assets around into new investments and recalculate the weighted average return on investment, we note that a slight alteration of assets can dramatically increase the weighted return—usually without any added risk.

Worksheet 12.3B demonstrates that by shifting $5,000 from a passbook savings account paying 5.25 percent to a money market fund paying 9.5 percent, Mr. Somebody's weighted average return would increase from 8.61 percent to 9.22 percent. If we project Mr. Somebody's $58,000 in assets out 25 years to his retirement at age 65, this small increase in the average rate of return would add an extra $70,000 to his total assets.

If Mr. Somebody wanted to take a larger risk and shifted that $5,000 into a discounted second mortgage paying 18.5 percent for the next 25 years, Worksheet 12.3C shows us he would add an additional two million dollars to his total assets. Such

is the power of compounding.

This analysis explains why Mr. Somebody must better position his current working assets because they are not working hard enough for him. When you make up your own worksheet, study it carefully and try to determine what risks can or must be taken for you to accumulate your desired levels of assets and income.

RANKING YOUR ASSETS

We now look at ranking the assets. Portfolios will vary according to individual nees. Worksheet 12.4 should help you become more conscious of what percentage of your investments are in risk-prone investments, and therefore more aware of how much risk you want to assume.

Any ranking system is going to be subjective, but using a computer makes it easy to tailor it so that it is meaningful to you. I prefer a simple ranking system, ranking assets from high to low:

1. Aggressive: commodities/speculative stocks, etc.
2. Quality: mutual funds/blue chip stocks/real estate, etc.
3. Conservative: government bonds/ bank CDs/money market funds.

A common way to visualize the ranking of

```
WORKSHEET  12.3ABC:  WEIGHTED AVERAGE RETURN ON INVESTMENTS


    MARGINS:   LEFT=3, RIGHT=85

    COLUMNS:   GLOBAL=14

    FORMAT:    COMMAS, NO DECIMALS

    PRINTER:   COMPRESS=OFF

    RUN AT:    YEAR END
```

WORKSHEET 12.3A: WEIGHTED AVERAGE RETURN ON INVESTMENTS

WORKSHEET INSTRUCTIONS: GO TO CELL A300

ASSUMPTIONS:

YEARS UNTIL RETIREMENT =   25

FUTURE INVESTMENT AMOUNT = $457,746

ASSETS	JANUARY AMOUNT	ESTIMATED RETURN	OF TOTAL RETURN	AVERAGE RETURN
SAVINGS	8,000	5.25%	13.55%	0.71%
STOCKS	6,500	9.00%	23.23%	2.09%
GOV'T BONDS	3,000	7.50%	19.35%	1.45%
REAL ESTATE	35,000	5.00%	12.90%	0.65%
IRA	5,500	12.00%	30.97%	3.72%
	$58,000	38.75%	100.00%	8.61%

WORKSHEET 12.3B: WEIGHTED AVERAGE RETURN ON INVESTMENTS

ASSUMPTIONS:

YEARS UNTIL RETIREMENT =   25

FUTURE INVESTMENT AMOUNT = $662,439

ASSETS	JANUARY AMOUNT	ESTIMATED RETURN	OF TOTAL RETURN	AVERAGE RETURN
SAVINGS	8,000	9.50%	24.52%	2.33%
STOCKS	6,500	9.00%	23.23%	2.09%
GOV'T BONDS	3,000	7.50%	19.35%	1.45%
REAL ESTATE	35,000	5.00%	12.90%	0.65%
IRA	5,500	12.00%	30.97%	3.72%
	$58,000	43.00%	110.97%	10.23%

WORKSHEET 12.3C: WEIGHTED AVERAGE RETURN ON INVESTMENTS

ASSUMPTIONS:

YEARS UNTIL RETIREMENT =   25

FUTURE INVESTMENT AMOUNT = $2,776,516

ASSETS	JANUARY AMOUNT	ESTIMATED RETURN	OF TOTAL RETURN	AVERAGE RETURN
SAVINGS	8,000	18.50%	47.74%	8.83%
STOCKS	6,500	9.00%	23.23%	2.09%
GOV'T BONDS	3,000	7.50%	19.35%	1.45%
REAL ESTATE	35,000	5.00%	12.90%	0.65%
IRA	5,500	12.00%	30.97%	3.72%
	$58,000	52.00%	134.19%	16.74%

assets is in the shape of a pyramid. The most aggressive and illiquid investments are at the top, where the pyramid is the smallest—a graphic indication that the smallest portion of your assets, if any, should be deployed there. The lowest level is the widest, representing the least risky, most liquid area. The largest portion of your assets usually will be found here.

There are two important considerations here. One, how much money do you put into each category? A conservative investor, who has modest long-term goals, might only put 20 percent of his net worth into aggressive stocks. A more aggressive investor, who has set high goals to achieve, and who is willing to accept the risk, might invest 50 percent of his net worth into speculative stocks.

The second consideration is which stocks and investments to buy. This is a subject to be discussed between you and your broker. Everyone who can afford to invest should probably have part of their portfolio in each of the three categories. It is a good idea to have an annual review of yoru assets and investment portfolio, to make sure its

elements are in the balance you wish. Updating this worksheet each year will be helpful in your annual review with your broker.

Worksheet 12.4 illustrates the concept of the investment pyramid. It shows Mr. and Mrs. Somebody's current assets, the amounts and the associated risk factors. An optional column for the desired percentage of assets could act as a guide or reminder in balancing your assets.

HISTORY OF ASSETS

Let's assume that you have maintained a history of your investments for the past five years. You now wish to use this information to forecast future growth of assets by preparing a worksheet that summarizes past growth and projects future growth for the next five years.

We can compute the growth rate for each year by using a simple percentage method:

Growth Rate = (Year 2 – Year 1)/Year 1

Next we assume that the estimated overall growth

WORKSHEET 12.4: RANKING YOUR ASSETS

MARGINS: LEFT=5, RIGHT=75

COLUMNS: GLOBAL 14

FORMAT: COMMAS, NO DECIMALS

SORT BY: RISK FACTOR

PRINTER: COMPRESS=OFF

RUN: AS NEEDED OR AT YEAR END

WORKSHEET 12.4: RANKING YOUR ASSETS

1.	AGGRESSIVE:	COMMODITY FUTURES	
		SPECULATIVE STOCK OPTIONS	
		OIL & GAS EXPLORATION	
2.	QUALITY:	MUTUAL FUNDS	
		BLUE CHIP STOCKS	
		REAL ESTATE	
3.	CONSERVATIVE:	TREASURY BILLS	
		BANK CD'S	
		MONEY MARKET FUNDS	

ASSET	AMOUNT	RISK FACTOR	PERCENT	DESIRED PERCENT
STOCK OPTIONS	6,500	1		
	$6,500	1	11.21%	
IRA	5,500	2		
REAL ESTATE	35,000	2		
	$40,500	2	69.83%	
GOV'T BONDS	3,000	3		
SAVINGS	$8,000	3		
	11,000	3	18.97%	
TOTAL ASSETS =	$58,000		100.00%	

91

rate is the average of the yearly rates. We can complete our five-year projection by multiplying the asset by its estimated growth rate.

Begin by retrieving your present list of assets from Worksheet 12.1. To these, add all the assets owned during the past five years which are not in your current portfolio. Worksheet 12.5 shows the estimated percent growth expected for each asset, and projects all current assets out five years. Movement of funds from one asset category to another

also should be reflected in the worksheet. In our example, Mr. Somebody transferred $2,000 from a mutual fund to an IRA in 1980.

Everything to the right of the middle vertical line is a projection of asset growth and will be calculated by the spreadsheet, i.e., 1984 to 1988. Again in our example, Mr. Somebody's savings account will grow by 5.25 percent each year. The formula for calculating the future value of this asset is as follows:

WORKSHEET   12.5:   HISTORY AND PROJECTION OF WORKING ASSETS

MARGINS: LEFT=2, RIGHT=132

COLUMNS: GLOBAL =10

FORMAT: COMMAS, NO DECIMALS

PRINTER: COMPRESS=ON

SORT BY: MAJOR CATEGORY

RUN AT: YEAR END

HISTORY   22-Oct-84

WORKSHEET 12.5:   HISTORY AND PROJECTION OF WORKING ASSETS   (ACTUAL VS PROJECTED)

ASSETS	ESTIMATED GROWTH RATE	ACTUAL (YEAR END)					PROJECTED (YEAR END)				
		1979	1980	1981	1982	1983	1984	1985	1986	1987	1988
SAVINGS	5.25%	5,500	6,000	6,500	7,300	8,000	8,420	8,862	9,327	9,817	10,332
STOCKS	9.00%	2,000	3,000	4,000	5,000	6,500	7,085	7,723	8,418	9,175	10,001
BONDS	7.50%	3,500	2,000	2,200	2,500	3,000	3,225	3,467	3,727	4,006	4,307
REAL ESTATE	5.00%	25,000	28,000	30,000	33,000	35,000	36,750	38,588	40,517	42,543	44,670
IRA	12.00%		2,200	4,400	4,900	5,500	6,160	6,899	7,727	8,654	9,693
MUTUAL FUND	15.00%	2,000									
MONEY MARKET	12.00%		1,000								
OIL/GAS	23.00%	2,000									
TOTAL NET WORTH =		$40,000	$42,200	$47,100	$52,700	$58,000	$61,640	$65,538	$69,716	$74,196	$79,003

Asset × (1 + Percent Return) ^ No. of Years

$8,000*(1.0525)^1

I recommend that you group your assets by major category: real estate, stocks, bonds. But there are a variety of other ways of grouping assets, for instance, by risk level, from low to speculative, by liquidity, and by a taxable or tax-free status.

After all the calculations are done and the formulas are copied throughout the worksheet, you could insert a one-position vertical column between your actual and projected asset forecast. This will make it easier to read.

PROJECTING ASSETS

Worksheet 12.6 makes some projections and demonstrates the effect of compound growth on our current assets. The forecasts are based on the assumption that all income from these assets (e.g., interest, dividends and realized capital gains) will be reinvested, presumably in the same type of investment, and will grow by a percentage return that you will select.

The percent return factor you choose should be your best estimate and reflect your personal goals. If you are conservative, make it 5 percent; if you are aggressive use 15 percent. If you are doubtful, compromise with 10 percent.

Once you've completed the worksheet, you'll know whether your assets are working hard enough to achieve your goals. If they are not, you either have to live with a revised goal or switch your assets into higher-yielding investments. In Worksheet 12.6, we see that the Somebodys' $58,000 in current assets will grow to almost $1 million in 25 years without any additional savings or contributions.

A quick way to set up this projection is to retrieve your current list of assets from one of the prior worksheets and group them by the estimated percentage return on the investment. Use absolute figures for current value and percent return when you copy your projection formula across your spreadsheet. Then use the EDIT command to change the number of years in each column of your future projections.

An example of the formula for calculating the future value of an asset is as follows:

Asset = $11,000, Return = 6 percent, Number of years = 5:

Assets × (1 + Percent Return) No. of years

(11,000)*(1.06)^5

WORKSHEET 12.6:   PROJECTING WORKING ASSETS

MARGINS: LEFT=3, RIGHT=85

COLUMNS: GLOBAL=12

FORMAT: COMMAS, NO DECIMALS

PRINTER: COMPRESS=OFF

RUN AT: YEAR END

WORKSHEET 12.6:   PROJECTING WORKING ASSETS

ASSETS	CURRENT VALUE	PERCENT RETURN	VALUE IN 5 YEARS	VALUE IN 10 YEARS	VALUE IN 25 YEARS
GOV'T BONDS	$3,000				
SAVINGS	$8,000				
	$11,000	6.00%	$14,720	$19,699	$47,211
IRA	$5,500				
REAL ESTATE	$35,000				
	$40,500	12.00%	$71,375	$125,787	$688,503
STOCKS	$6,500	15.00%	$13,074	$26,296	$213,973
TOTALS =	$58,000		$99,169	$171,782	$949,686

Tax Planning Model

Making money is half the battle in life. Keeping it is the other half. The more money you earn, the more taxes are applied to it. No matter how much money you make, it will rarely make you rich—not unless you learn how to lessen the IRS tax bite.

THE PLANNING MODEL

You are probably paying too much in taxes. The national average tax rate is 35 percent. If you add state tax to that average, most people are approaching the 50 percent tax bracket.

This means that for every dollar you earn, almost one-half goes to the government, and inflation erodes the buying power of the rest. Is there any question that we need to be aware of our tax situation? If, like most of us, you are in the 30 percent to 50 percent tax bracket, you can save thousands of dollars over the next few years simply be reducing your tax bracket.

Remember, there is nothing illegal about arranging your affairs to keep taxes as low as possible. Everyone has an obligation to pay his or her taxes. But no one is obliged to pay more than he must. A determined investor can always find investments that, at least partially, exclude the tax collector, and do so legally.

WHAT IS YOUR TAX BRACKET?

Most people have no idea what tax bracket they are in, much less understand how tax brackets are calculated.

Your federal income tax bracket, technically called your **marginal tax rate,** is the percentage of income tax you pay on the highest part of your taxable income. Your taxable income is the total income you report, minus all exemptions, exclusions, adjustments to income, and deductions.

For example, our married couple, Mr. and Mrs. Somebody, filed a joint return showing a taxable income of $35,597 for 1983 and paid $6,763 in federal income tax. They were taxed $6,624 on their first $35,200 of taxable income and 35 percent ($139) on the $397 by which their taxable income exceeded $35,200.

FIGURE 13.1:   1984 FEDERAL TAX RATES
===
FOR MARRIED TAXPAYERS FILING A JOINT RETURN
IF YOUR TAXABLE INCOME IS

MORE THAN	BUT LESS THAN	YOUR HIGHEST MARGINAL TAX RATE IS
0	3,400	0.00%
3,400	5,500	11.00%
5,500	7,600	12.00%
7,600	11,900	14.00%
11,900	16,000	16.00%
16,000	20,200	18.00%
20,200	24,600	22.00%
24,600	29,900	25.00%
29,900	35,200	28.00%
35,200	45,800	33.00%
45,800	60,000	38.00%
60,000	85,600	42.00%
85,600	109,400	45.00%
109,400	162,400	49.00%
162,400	–	50.00%

FOR SINGLE TAXPAYERS
IF YOUR TAXABLE INCOME IS

MORE THAN	BUT LESS THAN	YOUR HIGHEST MARGINAL TAX RATE IS
0	2,300	0.00%
2,300	3,400	11.00%
3,400	4,400	12.00%
4,400	6,500	14.00%
6,500	8,500	15.00%
8,500	10,800	16.00%
10,800	12,900	18.00%
12,900	15,000	20.00%
15,000	18,200	23.00%
18,200	23,500	26.00%
23,500	28,800	30.00%
28,800	34,100	34.00%
34,100	41,500	38.00%
41,500	55,300	42.00%
55,300	81,800	48.00%
81,800	–	50.00%

Even though their $6,624 tax amounted to 19 percent of their $35,597 taxable income, they were in the 35 percent bracket because their top income was subject to that 35 percent bite.

Since we are using a typical American couple, we have to remember to add state tax to their federal tax. In California, for instance, the maximum state tax is up to 11 percent of taxable income, or approximately 20 percent of the maximum federal tax. In our example, we therefore add a state tax of 7 percent to the 33 percent and arrive at 40 percent. We now can say that in 1983, the couple was in the 40 percent income tax bracket.

The tax bracket is a very important number. This is the number that governs investment decisions. You have to learn to think in after-tax return. Do Mr. and Mrs. Somebody want investments that yield them more taxable income since on each additional dollar of taxable income they pay 40 cents over to the government? Or does our couple want investments which yield more income tax deductions? On each one dollar of deductions they can reduce their taxes by 40 cents.

How much taxable income does it take to be in the 50 percent tax bracket today? The tax rate table below shows us that in 1984, a couple earning $60,000 of taxable income is in the 42 percent federal tax bracket. If we add the usual percentage for state tax, they would be over the 50 percent tax bracket. In other words, it is not difficult at all for a couple working full time to be in the 50 percent tax bracket.

YOUR BASIC TAX MODEL

The purpose of the rest of this chapter is to simplify income taxes and to motivate you to take action to reduce them. The first worksheet we will deal with is a simple, one-page report which can save you thousands of dollars over the next few years. It is a model of your tax return. I call it the Basic Tax Model.

A vital part of your personal money management is a year-by-year comparison of your income tax returns. The Basic Tax Model is simply a summary of your tax returns over the past five years. Its beauty lies in its simplicity. It is a snapshot of

your taxes, but without all the unnecessary detail. In fact, the simpler you make this report, the better. Its purpose is to help you understand the basic structure of the federal tax code. Once you understand its basic design, you will find it much easier to save on your taxes.

One of the benefits of constructing the Tax Model is a greater awareness of those tax deductions that really count. It can help you look for investment opportunities that maximize your wealth and minimize your taxes.

Your Basic Tax Model can be as simple as listing the four major categories of your federal tax return. In fact, I recommend that you begin your spreadsheet with these four major categories: total income, adjusted gross, taxable income, and net tax.

SETTING UP YOUR BASIC TAX MODEL

The first step is to assemble your federal and state tax returns for the past five years and identify the various kinds of income and deductions. Then set up the tax model for one year as illustrated in Worksheet 13.1. Enter your figures for Total Income. If you are using the 1983 Income Tax Return Form 1040 as a guide, total income can be found on Line 22. Next put in your net tax figure—called Total Tax on Line 56 of your Form 1040—your Adjusted Gross Income (Line 32) and your Total Taxable Income (Line 37).

At the bottom of the model, add your federal and state tax paid to arrive at Total Taxes Paid. Then divide this number by Total Income to calculate the Paid Rate. Our marginal tax rate comes from the federal and state tax tables. Add them together to get your combined effective tax rate or tax bracket.

Worksheet 13.1 illustrates the Basic Tax Model, using Mr. and Mrs. Somebody's 1983 tax return.

HOW THE TAX MODEL WORKS

A vital part of your personal money management is a year-by-year comparison of your income tax returns. Worksheet 13.2 expands on the Basic

WORKSHEET 13.1: YOUR BASIC TAX MODEL

MARGINS: LEFT=3, RIGHT=85

COLUMNS: GLOBAL=10, A=3, B=17

FORMAT: COMMAS,NO DECIMALS

PRINTER: COMPRESS=OFF

RUN: QUARTERLY

TAXMODEL   22-Oct-84

WORKSHEET 13.1:   YOUR BASIC TAX MODEL

==

1. TOTAL INCOME = $47,700

----

2. ADJUSTED GROSS = $43,637

----

3. TAXABLE INCOME = $35,597

----

4. TOTAL TAX: FEDERAL = $6,763
                    STATE = $1,353

                TOTAL TAXES = $8,116

TOTAL TAXES/TOTAL INCOME =   17.01%

TAX BRACKET: FEDERAL =   35.00%
                    STATE =   7.00%

          TOTAL TAX BRACKET = 42.00%

Tax Model to include the past five years of tax returns.

The worksheet shows us that like most people, our couple, Mr. and Mrs. Somebody, have not taken advantage of all of the tax shelters that they could have used. Mrs. Somebody had some home business expenses as well as some investment tax credit for new office equipment, but only Mr. Somebody took advantage of an IRA or Keogh account.

The Tax Model also show us that while the Somebody's total income increased from $22,146 to $47,700 (115 percent over 5 years), their total tax increased 155 percent. This is because as they earned more money they were pushed into a higher tax bracket, and they were able to keep less and less of what they earned.

Worksheet 13.2 gives us a closer look at the Somebody's itemized tax returns, using the five-year tax model as our format. Our next topic will concern ways to save on taxes.

HOW TO USE THE TAX MODEL TO REDUCE YOUR TAXES

There are two primary ways to save on taxes. The first is by lowering taxes on income, primarily by shifting from short-term to long-term profits. The second is by reducing taxable income, primarily by making use of tax shelters. This discussion will focus on the latter.

Let's assume that you would like to reduce your tax bracket and improve your net worth. There are several things that you can do to improve your situation.

Rule No. 1: the sooner you take deductions on the Basic Tax Model, the better. Where most taxpayers go wrong is that they concentrate on the wrong tax deductions. They wait to reduce taxable income by itemizing their deductions, instead of concentrating on those deductions that reduce total income. An awareness of this one fact can save you hundreds of tax dollars.

For example, assume that your adjusted gross income is $16,000, and you spend $1,000 for medical care. In 1983, you are allowed to deduct only those expenses that exceeded 5 percent of your adjusted gross income (i.e., $16,000 × 5% = $800). So $1,000 in cash expenses results in only $200 of deductions. Had you earned $20,000 or more, you would not be allowed to deduct any of your $1,000 of medical expenses.

Taxpayers who wait until Schedule A to itemize deductions are missing out on dozens of tax opportunities. Most itemized deductions are not worth much. That is why Schedule A is often called the schedule of last resort.

Rule No. 2: convert low-leverage investments to high-leverage investments. Since interest payments are tax deductible, you should not be afraid to borrow, whenever the leverage offered by borrowing can multiply your wealth, and you have the ability to repay the loan. Remember that

```
WORKSHEET  13.2:    EXAMPLE OF THE TAX MODEL

MARGINS:   LEFT=3, RIGHT=85

COLUMNS:   GLOBAL=10, A=20

FORMAT:    COMMAS, NO DECIMALS

PRINTER:   COMPRESS=OFF

RUN AT:    THIRD QUARTER AND YEAR END
```

WORKSHEET 13.2:   EXAMPLE OF THE TAX MODEL

GROSS INCOME	1979	1980	1981	1982	1983
Salary	22,000	25,000	26,000	27,000	31,000
Interest	175	200	225	250	300
Dividend	75	150	250	350	400
State tax refund	121	105	412	398	412
Business income	(225)	(1,430)	9,538	10,780	15,000
Property income	0	(1,510)	(1,535)	(1,588)	(1,592)
Capital gains	0	4,991	1,778	1,602	2,180
1. TOTAL INCOME	22,146	27,506	36,668	38,792	47,700

DEDUCTIONS

	1979	1980	1981	1982	1983
Move expenses	0	1,695	1,567	0	0
Business expense	0	1,485	1,197	1,562	2,063
IRA/KEOGH	0	0	0	0	2,000
2. ADJUSTED GROSS	22,146	24,326	33,904	37,230	43,637
Medical expenses	78	65	96	103	147
State sales tax	1,054	1,024	1,030	1,079	1,099
Interest expense	5,448	5,376	5,217	5,146	5,108
Charity	588	350	318	376	385
Misc deductions	415	586	690	756	701
Zero tax bracket	(3,400)	(3,400)	(3,400)	(3,400)	(3,400)
Exemptions x 1000	4,000	4,000	4,000	4,000	4,000
3. TAXABLE INCOME	13,963	16,325	25,953	29,170	35,597
Total tax	2,709	3,353	4,937	4,052	6,763
Tax credit	60	40	126	0	0
4. TAXES:FEDERAL=	$2,649	$3,313	$4,811	$5,052	$6,763
STATE =	$530	$663	$962	$1,010	$1,353
TOTAL TAXES =	$3,179	$3,976	$5,773	$6,062	$8,116
TAXES/INCOME =	14.35%	14.45%	15.74%	15.63%	17.01%

TAX BRACKET:

	1979	1980	1981	1982	1983
FEDERAL =	19.00%	19.00%	30.00%	30.00%	35.00%
STATE =	3.80%	3.80%	6.00%	6.00%	7.00%
TOTAL =	22.80%	22.80%	36.00%	36.00%	42.00%

the tax benefits you get with your new investments can be pocketed now to help with the investment payments, and therefore actually reduce them.

Rule No. 3: convert single-benefit investments to multiple-benefit investments. If you have a savings account, for example, you could put part of it into an IRA or Keogh retirement plan and get a nice tax break as well as some tax deferred income.

These are just some examples of how you can lessen the IRS tax bite. Not all or necessarily any of these will apply to your situation. The illustration is merely to stimulate your thinking. Through careful, intelligent research, you will be able to discover many more ways to keep more of what you earn.

DO-IT-YOURSELF TAX PLANNING

Worksheet 13.3 shows Mr. Somebody's tax model for last year and projects what it might be for next year.

When should this tax model be complete? Since we can control the taxes we pay, this tax forecast should be completed before the year's end. At the end of October, you have 10 months of actual information about your tax liability. Enter in this 10 months of information. Add to this your best estimate for the months of November and December. Now you have a very good picture of your 1984 tax liability and enough time left to take action to reduce your income taxes before year's end.

When you construct your forecasting model, it is not necessary to add all the detail from last year's tax return, but only enough to find out where you are most liable. Once you've done this, then review your worksheet with your tax advisor. Only in this way can you get the deductions to cover the income you intend to make.

One final caveat: don't go overboard to save taxes. Everyone likes to save on taxes, but tax savings alone should never be the sole factor in any financial decision. A tax shelter should be a sound business venture. Remember, with any investment think of economics first, taxes last.

TAX SHELTER INVESTMENTS

Some people don't need to worry much about the tax implications of their investments. Others put tax considerations first, investment considerations last. Still other people who really would benefit from tax-sheltered investments have not done so because they don't know how much of their investment return is going to Uncle Sam, or they don't know how to evaluate tax-shelter investments.

Anyone who has purchased a home owns a tax shelter because the interest expense and real estate taxes on the property are tax-deductible. When you sell your home, profits are usually taxed at the lower long-term capital gains rate, if at all. Worksheet 13.4 turns your personal computer into a tax planning system for evaluating tax reduction strategies. It is a simple model that uses various alternative investments to reveal the net cost of these investments and the effect on your taxable income.

The information about your income for your current year's taxable income and tax bracket are entered at the top of the worksheet. The total tax

due is taken from last year's federal and state tax tables if you don't have this year's tables.

The amount of the investment and the first year's write-off are entered as a percent or dollar amount. Subtract the first year's write-off from your taxable income to get the next taxable income after investment. Again compute your total taxes due from the tax tables. The net savings is the difference between total tax due before and after the investment. To this savings you add investment tax

WORKSHEET 13.3: PROJECTION OF INCOME TAXES

MARGINS: LEFT=4, RIGHT=75

COLUMNS: GLOBAL=12, A=25

FORMAT: COMMAS, NO DECIMALS

PRINTER: COMPRESS=OFF

RUN: QUARTERLY

WORKSHEET   13.3   PROJECTION OF INCOME TAXES

```
----------------------------------------------
GROSS INCOME            1983        1984
----------------------------------------------

Salary                31,000      34,100
Interest                 300         325
Dividend                 400         425
State tax refund         412         450
Business income       15,000      17,500
Property income       (1,592)     (2,000)
Capital gains          2,180       2,200
----------------------------------------------
1. TOTAL INCOME       47,700      53,000

DEDUCTIONS
-----------------

Move expenses              0           0
Business expense       2,063       2,200
IRA/KEOGH              2,000       4,000
----------------------------------------------
2. ADJUSTED GROSS     43,637      46,800


Medical expenses         147         200
State sales tax        1,099       1,200
Interest expense       5,108       5,200
Charity                  385         425
Misc deductions          701         775
Zero tax bracket      (3,400)     (3,400)
Exemptions x 1000      4,000       4,000
----------------------------------------------
3. TAXABLE INCOME     35,597      38,400

Total tax              6,763       7,330
Tax credit                 0           0
----------------------------------------------
4.  TAXES:FEDERAL=    $6,763      $7,330
          STATE =     $1,353      $1,466
                     --------    --------
     TOTAL TAXES =    $8,116      $8,796

  TAXES/INCOME  =      17.01%      16.60%


     TAX BRACKET:
        FEDERAL =      35.00%      33.00%
          STATE =      7.00%       6.60%
                     --------    --------
          TOTAL =     42.00%      39.60%
```

```
WORKSHEET 13.4:   TAX SAVINGS WORKSHEET

MARGINS:   LEFT=5, RIGHT=85

COLUMNS:   GLOBAL=10, A=25

FORMAT:    COMMAS, NO DECIMALS

PRINTER:   COMPRESS=OFF

RUN:       AS NEEDED
```

TAXSAVE   22-Oct-84

WORKSHEET 13.4:   TAX SAVINGS WORKSHEET

==

WITHOUT INVESTMENT:

   TAXABLE INCOME = $35,597

      TAX BRACKET =   40.00%

         TAX DUE = $8,116

WITH INVESTMENT:	ALTERNATIVE NO. 1		ALTERNATIVE NO. 2	
AMOUNT OF INVESTMENT =		$10,000		$10,000
FIRST YEAR WRITE-OFF =	45.00%	$4,500	40.00%	$4,000
NET TAXABLE INCOME AFTER INVESTMENT =		$31,097		$31,597
NET TAX SAVINGS =		$1,800		$1,600
TAX DUE =		$6,316		$6,516
INVESTMENT TAX CREDIT =	5.00%	$500	10.00%	$1,000
TOTAL TAX SAVINGS =		$2,300		$2,600

NET COST OF INVESTMENT:

	ALTERNATIVE NO. 1	ALTERNATIVE NO. 2
AMOUNT INVESTED =	$10,000	$10,000
LESS TAXES SAVED =	$2,300	$2,600
NET COST OF INVESTMENT =	$7,700	$7,400
PERCENT RETURN ON INVESTMENT	77.00%	74.00%

credits to get total tax savings.

The net cost of the investment would be the amount of money invested less total taxes saved. The percent return on the investment is computed by dividing the net cost by the amount invested. If the investment calls for payments and tax write-offs over several years, you should make an estimate of effects in those years also.

Life Insurance

The purpose of insurance is to cover medical expenses and to meet financial obligations when the policy holder—either through disability or death—cannot.

As income and financial responsibility increase, you should buy additional insurance to adjust death benefits accordingly. On the other hand, as you grow older you may wish to withdraw the cash value of your policies, as you no longer need the family protections you once did.

HOW MUCH LIFE INSURANCE IS ENOUGH?

How much insurance do you need? There is no easy answer to this question because so many other factors must be considered: goals, net worth, future expenses, income, and family needs. Every family or individual needs a different amount of insurance. However, there are a number of accepted, fundamental approaches to the question.

As a rule of thumb, insurance experts suggest life policies with proceeds totaling four to five times annual salary. This means, in the case of Mr. Somebody earning $31,000 per year, that his insurance requirements would be somewhere between $124,000 and $155,000.

How is this figure arrived at? While there can be differences among individuals, the procedure is a matter of simple arithmetic. Essentially, it is just a matter of determining earning power under normal life expectancy.

Since Mr. Somebody at age 40 is earning $31,000, he will earn more than $775,000 in gross income over the next 25 years until he retires at age 65 (31,000 × 25 = $775,000). This assumes no further increases in salary and no additional income from other sources. From this we will subtract 20 percent, which normally goes toward taxes. We also subtract his Social Security benefits because these benefits will reduce the family's need for insurance protection. The Social Security benefits are estimated to be approximately $10,000 per year, making his net annual required earnings for the next 25 years equal $370,000.

$775,000 × 20 percent = $620,000

less ($10,000 × 25 years) = $370,000

If we divide $370,000 by 25 years we get $14,800 per year, which would replace that $370,00 net earnings figure, except that it hasn't taken into consideration the present value of the dollar for those 25 years. To do that, the $14,800 must be multiplied by a factor known as the net present value of the dollar, at what currently is considered a reasonable, long-rate rate of interest; such a reasonable rate might be 10 percent, or you can choose any value you think reasonable. This process is called discounting the present value of your money.

Lotus 1-2-3 has a built-in function that automatically will compute net present value. The form of this function is:

@NPV (Discount Rate * Range)

The discount rate is the assumed interest rate over a number of years, and the range is the stream of funds to be discounted, usually represented by a series of rows or columns. Use the /DATA FILE function to develop your range. Set the range equal to the number of years until retirement. Start with the amount required per year (e.g., $14,800). Step by 0, stop at any number higher than $14,800. In our example we included the range in column G of our worksheet.

@NPV(.10 * G10 . . . G34)

In Worksheet 14.1, the NPV function produces $134,340. In other words, $134,340 invested at 10 percent interest will provide an annual cash return equal to the Somebodys' $14,800 income requirement for the next 25 years. This is Mr. Somebody's economic value to his family and his

107

```
          WORKSHEET  14.1:  HOW MUCH LIFE INSURANCE

          MARGINS:  LEFT=5, RIGHT=85

          COLUMNS:  GLOBAL=9

          FORMAT:   PERCENT, 2 DECIMALS

          PRINTER:  COMPRESS=OFF

          RUN AT:   YEAR END
```

LIFEINS   22-Oct-84

WORKSHEET 14.1:   HOW MUCH LIFE INSURANCE DO YOU NEED?

			FORMULA RANGE	NUMBER OF
			G10...G34	YEARS
SOMEBODY'S SALARY =		$31,000		
			14,800	1
RULE OF THUMB:			14,800	2
			14,800	3
($31,000 x 4) =		$124,000	14,800	4
or			14,800	5
($31,000 x 5) =		$155,000	14,800	6
			14,800	7
SOMEBODY'S AGE =	40		14,800	8
			14,800	9
YEARS TO RETIREMENT=	25		14,800	10
(AGE 65)			14,800	11
			14,800	12
FUTURE GROSS EARNINGS =		$775,000	14,800	13
(25 YEARS x $31,000)			14,800	14
			14,800	15
LESS FEDERAL & STATE TAXES =		$155,000	14,800	16
(APPROXIMATELY 20%)			14,800	17
			14,800	18
LESS SOC SEC BENEFITS =		$250,000	14,800	19
($10,000 x 25 YEARS)			14,800	20
			14,800	21
NET FUTURE EARNINGS =		$370,000	14,800	22
			14,800	23
			14,800	24
DIVIDED BY YEARS TO RETIRE =		$14,800	14,800	25
($370,000 / 25 YEARS)				

```
LIFE INSURANCE NEEDED =        $134,340
   "@NPV(.10%, G10..G34)        ==========
```

present life insurance requirement. Note that the insurance amount required is approximately four to five times his annual salary.

This insurance amount may gradually decrease due to the fact that as each year goes by, there is one less year for which income must be provided. Mrs. Somebody's potential earnings also will reduce the need for insurance protection. Further, assets will be building in the estate in some other forms such as retirement plans, pension plans, and investment portfolio. All of these factors could provide income for the surviving family.

ESTIMATING YOUR IMMEDIATE CASH REQUIREMENTS

If your family is dependent upon you, you must consider how they will be cared for after you die. Since death may come at any time, you must consider what your dependents' need would be if you were to die now, not 10 or 20 years from now. You can use worksheet 14.2 as a planning model to determine your family's financial needs after your death and the sources of income to meet those needs. You can then use insurance to make up the difference between the two.

Worksheet 14.2 illustrates the needs and income that the Somebody family predicted for themselves if James Somebody were to die now. The prediction is based on five factors.

1. Funeral Expenses. Estimate these at about 10 percent of your gross income. James Somebody's gross was $31,000, so they estimated expenses to be $3,000.

2. Mortgages and short-term bills. Determine the amount of money to be paid off at your death. All of these bills and debts should be resolved at your death, so that your family does not have to worry about maintaining credit relationships. The home mortgage can be considered a separate debt and handled differently. You can either buy a mortgage term policy to pay off this debt if you die, or include the annual mortgage payment in an assessment of your family's annual living expense needs.

3. Estate Taxes. This should include all estate taxes, probate costs and administrative expenses. Your gross estate is valued at the date of your death. After subtracting allowable deductions, your net estate is then subject to federal estate taxes. The estate tax ranges from 18 percent at the lowest level to 50 percent for estates larger than $2.5 million. The 50 percent top estate rate starts in 1985. The following table shows the tax on estates of various sizes:

Taxable Estate	Marginal Estate Tax Rate (percent)	Estimated Tax
$150,000	32	$38,800
$500,000	37	$155,800
$1,000,000	41	$345,800
$2,500,000	Varies	$1,025,800

```
WORKSHEET  14.2:  LIFE INSURANCE PLANNER

MARGINS:   LEFT=5, RIGHT=75

COLUMNS:   A=30, C=12

FORMAT:    COMMAS, NO DECIMALS

PRINTER:   COMPRESS=OFF

RUN AT:    YEAR END
```

WORKSHEET 14.2: LIFE INSURANCE PLANNING

IMMEDIATE CASH REQUIREMENTS	AMOUNT
FUNERAL EXPENSES	$3,000
MORTGAGES & SHORT TERM BILLS	$2,000
ESTATE TAXES, PROBATE COSTS	$15,000
CURRENT LIVING EXPENSES	$5,000
COLLEGE EDUCATION FUND	$20,000
TOTAL REQUIRED =	$45,000

CASH IMMEDIATELY AVAILABLE	AMOUNT
LIFE INSURANCE PROCEEDS	$150,000
COMPANY DEATH BENEFIT PAYMENTS	$50,000
OTHER BENEFITS	$25,000
TOTAL AVAILABLE =	$225,000
NET CASH AVAILABLE =	$180,000

Mr. Somebody's taxable estate is estimated to be less than $100,000, so his tax is estimated at $15,000.

4. Current Living Expenses. Estimate the amount of money your family will need for immediate daily use if you die. You probably cannot predict all the expenses that might surround your death, but a contingency fund equal to twice your current monthly take-home pay is normally sufficient. James Somebody earns $2,500 each month, so his contingency fund should be $5,000.

5. College Education Fund. Estimate how much it will cost to provide educational funds for your children and to send them to college. The Somebody's have decided that $20,000 invested to-day will produce enough funds for four years of state-supported schooling for both their children. The next chapter will deal with the subject of education in more depth.

CASH IMMEDIATELY AVAILABLE

Following are factors to be considered when calculating funds available upon a family member's death.

1. Life Insurance Proceeds. This can be determined by adding up the face amounts payable from all your life insurance policies. Jim and Judy Somebody both have term life policies payable to each other upon the death of the spouse. Mr. Somebody has an $150,000 policy and Judy

Somebody a $50,000 policy.

2. Company Death Benefits. Many times employers will provide group life insurance and survivor benefit plans for their employees. In the event of your death, they usually pay a monthly income for a limited period of time to your survivors. Mr. Somebody estimates that SMC Corporation's benefits will total $50,000.

3. Other Benefits. This category would include liquid assets and Social Security benefits paid to dependent children under the age of 18. The Somebodys estimate these benefits will total $25,000.

You should re-evaluate Worksheet 14.2 periodically. All of these sources of income and cash requirements will change, so it is important that you keep up to date with changes and how they will affect you. What may be adequate to meet your needs today may be inadequate five years from now.

Education Planning

In 1962, when I enrolled at a California state college, tuition was $48 a semester. In 1975, when I went back to a private university to get an M.B.A. degree, tuition was $52 per credit unit (about $2,000 per year). To take these same graduate classes in 1985, I would have to pay $185 per credit unit (or about $8,000 per year). That's a 300 percent increase over the past 10 years alone. No wonder parents fear that education could be their largest expense.

EDUCATION COSTS

Most parents feel a moral obligation to provide their children with the best possible education. Education costs become, in many instances, a need that partially overrides lifestyle preferences. Consider this: you have two young children. It now costs $20,000 to put a child through four years of a public college. Fifteen years from now, assuming inflation averages 6 percent a year, it will cost $48,000 per child!

Remember, education costs are not tax deductible. They must be paid for with expensive after-tax dollars unless careful planning is utilized.

Providing for this increasingly expensive obligation becomes part of a long-term plan. The earlier the funding begins, the lesser the burden.

Worksheet 15.1 helps to illustrate this planning exercise with our hypothetical family, Mr. and Mrs. Somebody and their two children, Jack and Jill, ages 6 and 10.

We start by listing the children, their ages and the number of years until they plan to start college (1993 for Jill and 1996 for Jack). We enter today's average cost ($20,000) for a four-year college education. Then we factor in an assumed rate of inflation and multiply that rate by the number of years before the children will be starting college (8 years for Jill and 12 years for Jack). This gives us the total college costs for both children in future dollars.

In our example, the formulas for Jill and Jack, assuming a 5 percent rate of inflation, would be:

WORKSHEET 15.1:   EDUCATION CONSIDERATIONS

MARGINS: LEFT=5, RIGHT=75

COLUMNS: GLOBAL=13

FORMAT: COMMAS, NO DECIMALS

PRINTER: COMPRESS=OFF

RUN AT: YEAR END

EDCONSID   22-Oct-84

WORKSHEET   15.1   EDUCATION CONSIDERATIONS

CHILDREN AND AGES	YEARS TIL COLLEGE	TODAY'S COLLEGE COSTS	EXPECTED RATE OF INFLATION	TOTAL COLLEGE COST
JACK = 6	12	$20,000	5.00%	$35,917
JILL =10	8	$20,000	5.00%	$29,549
		TOTAL TUITION COSTS =		$65,466

$$(\$20,000)*(1.05)^8$$

and

$$(\$20,000)*(1.05)^{12}.$$

FUTURE EDUCATION NEEDS

Worksheet 15.2 helps us project education costs on a year-by-year basis. It uses the assumptions and calculations from Worksheet 15.1 and shows us what the educational costs will be during the actual years the children are in college. It also will total those costs by year for both children and show us the cumulative amount of funds required in future dollars.

We start by listing the years that Jill and Jack will be in college (1993 to 1996 for Jill and 1996 to 1999 for Jack). It also helps to indicate the year number (numbering from this year), that these costs will be incurred. For example, numbering from 1985, Jill is expected to be in college during the ninth through the 12th years, and Jack will be enrolled from the 12th through the 15th year. This gives us a very graphic picture of how many years the Somebodys have to accumulate the funds for their children's education.

We then decide how much the college education will cost per year (e.g., $20,000 / 4 years = $5,000 per year) and use our formula to calculate what that cost will be in future dollars for the re-

```
WORKSHEET  15.2:   EDUCATION  NEEDS


MARGINS:   LEFT=3,  RIGHT=132

COLUMNS:   GLOBAL=12

FORMAT:    COMMAS,  NO DECIMALS

PRINTER:   COMPRESS=OFF

RUN AT:    BEGINNING OF YEAR
```

EDNEEDS   22-Oct-84

WORKSHEET 15.2   EDUCATION NEEDS - DISTRIBUTED IN FUTURE DOLLARS

YEAR	1993	1994	1995	1996	1997	1998	1999
YEAR #	9	10	11	12	13	14	15
JILL	$7,757	$8,144	$8,552	$8,979			
JACK				$8,979	$9,428	$9,900	$10,395
TOTALS	$7,757	$8,144	$8,552	$17,959	$9,428	$9,900	$10,395
CUMULATE	$7,757	$15,901	$24,453	$42,411	$51,840	$61,739	$72,134

quired years. In the case of Jill, her four year college cost would be calculated as follows, assuming an inflation rate of 5 percent:

$$1993 = (\$5,000)*(1.05)^9$$
$$1994 = (\$5,000)*(1.05)^{10}$$
$$1995 = (\$5,000)*(1.05)^{11}$$
$$1996 = (\$5,000)*(1.05)^{12}$$

Jack's four-year college costs would be:

$$1996 = (\$5,000)*(1.05)^{12}$$
$$1997 = (\$5,000)*(1.05)^{13}$$
$$1998 = (\$5,000)*(1.05)^{14}$$
$$1999 = (\$5,000)*(1.05)^{15}$$

BEATING THE HIGH COST OF COLLEGE TUITION

Despite the cuts in federal student assistance programs and the rapid tuition jumps at public and private colleges, parents and students need not feel cut off from the opportunities of a higher education. All it takes is better and longer planning.

Worksheet 15.3 helps us plan how to invest our funds to meet the education costs for our children. It builds on and uses the information derived from the two previous worksheets.

It assumes that we will give each child a certain sum of money to be invested for his or her future college education. It also assumes that the

WORKSHEET   15.3:   PROJECTION OF EDUCATION FUNDS

MARGINS: LEFT=3, RIGHT=85

COLUMNS: GLOBAL=10, A=4, B=7

FORMAT: COMMAS, NO DECIMALS

PRINTER: COMPRESS=OFF

RUN AT: BEGINNING OF YEAR

EDFUNDS   22-Oct-84

WORKSHEET 15.3:   PROJECTION OF EDUCATION FUNDS

ASSUMPTIONS:

	AMOUNT OF GIFT	RATE OF RETURN
GIFT TO JILL =	$10,000	12.00%
GIFT TO JACK =	$10,000	10.50%

YEAR #	YEAR	JILL EARNS	JILL WITHDRAWS	JILL'S TOTAL	JACK EARNS	JACK WITHDRAWS	JACK'S TOTAL
1	1985	1,200		11,200	1,050		11,050
2	1986	1,344		12,544	1,160		12,210
3	1987	1,505		14,049	1,282		13,492
4	1988	1,686		15,735	1,417		14,909
5	1989	1,888		17,623	1,565		16,474
6	1990	2,115		19,738	1,730		18,204
7	1991	2,369		22,107	1,911		20,116
8	1992	2,653		24,760	2,112		22,228
9	1993	2,971	7,757	19,974	2,334		24,562
10	1994	2,397	8,144	14,227	2,579		27,141
11	1995	1,707	8,552	7,382	2,850		29,991
12	1996	886	8,979	(711)	3,149	$8,979	24,161
13	1997				2,537	$9,428	17,269
14	1998				1,813	$9,900	9,183
15	1999				964	$10,395	(248)

money will grow at an expected rate of return. It then takes the required funds needed for both children's college education from Worksheet 15.2 and calculates whether the invested funds will adequately cover the anticipated college costs.

In our example on Worksheet 15.3, we assume that Mr. Somebody will give a gift of $10,000 to each of his children in 1985. The worksheet shows, year by year, exactly how much each gift will grow if invested at an expected rate of return. It also shows a running total of the invested funds.

The worksheet is constructed so that you can change the amount of money given to either child and the expected rate of return. The Year and Year # columns help us visualize how the invested funds cumulate and how they are distributed during the college years.

CONSTRUCTING AN EDUCATION MODEL

In this example, we place the figures for the gift amount for each child and the rate of return for each child in a parameter table at the top of the worksheet. You can prepare an alternative scenario for your college fund by simple changing the amounts or percentages in the table.

Use Lotus 1-2-3's DATA FILL function to enter the starting line number, the starting year,

the range, and the step by one each year. Jill's first year's earnings are calculated by multiplying the amount of the gift times the rate of return ($10,000 × 12 percent). The amount is placed in Jill's Total column. The second and all succeeding year's earnings are computed as follows:

Jill's Total × Absolute Rate of Return

Copy this formula down Jill's Total column to the start of her freshman year (1993). Jack's earnings are calculated the same way using his rate of return (10.5 percent).

The Funds Withdrawn amounts are the expected college costs per year and are keyed from Worksheet 15.2. They represent the annual total dollars needed for both Jack's and Jill's education.

These withdrawal amounts are subtracted from Jack's or Jill's totals after computing their interest earned. In Worksheet 15.3, for example, Jill's freshman (1993) year's formula is:

Jill's Total = Interest Earned + prior Year's Amount − Withdrawal

$19,974 = ($24,760 × 12 percent) + $24,760 − $7,757

It is a good idea to add a horizontal window at the bottom of your screen so that as you experiment with different gift amounts and rates of return for each child, you can see if the investments cover the college costs.

The Challenge of Retirement

Just as you prepare in school for your career years, you should prepare now for your retirement years. Recent medical and scientific advances are making it possible for more people to stay healthier and live longer, and increasing numbers of people are including early retirement in their long-range plans.

WHY PLAN FOR RETIREMENT?

As a result, more people now spend a significant portion of their lives in retirement. The following worksheets are designed to help you prepare for your future by introducing you to some of the important elements of retirement planning.

These worksheets are not designed to give specific answers. Instead, they are intended to stimulate your thinking about your personal retirement plans. Worksheet 16.1 assists you in estimating your retirement income and expenses. Worksheet 16.2 will help you obtain financial independence at retirement.

Figuring out your projected cash flow at retirement is not as hard as it sounds. Start by listing your present sources of income from your Personal Budget Worksheet 10.1. The estimate of your retirement income could be based on such things as your company's annual benefits statement and your statement of earnings from the Social Security Administration.

Precise figures are not required because you will be reworking these amounts from time to time in order to take into account changes in your salary, pension, and social security benefits.

Your estimated retirement expenses should be grouped into several major categories like those shown in Worksheet 16.1. You'd also be wise to include an estimate of the taxes that will be paid on your retirement income.

INCOME NEEDED FOR RETIREMENT

When wage and price controls were enacted in 1973, inflation was out of control and running at the unheard of rate of 3 percent per year. Stop and consider this: Mr. Somebody is 25 years from retirement. He knows he could live comfortably on

WORKSHEET 16.1:   ESTIMATED RETIREMENT INCOME & EXPENSES

MARGINS: LEFT=5, RIGHT=75

COLUMNS: GLOBAL=12, A=20

FORMAT: COMMAS, NO DECIMALS

PRINTER: COMPRESS=OFF

RUN AT: YEAR END

RETEXP   22-Oct-84

WORKSHEET 16.1:   ESTIMATED RETIREMENT INCOME AND EXPENSES

MONTHLY INCOME	PRESENT INCOME	RETIREMENT INCOME
SALARY	$3,580	$0
INTEREST	$300	$550
DIVIDENDS	$400	$650
PENSION		$1,200
SOCIAL SECURITY		$900
TOTALS =	$4,280	$3,300

MONTHLY EXPENSES	PRESENT EXPENSES	RETIREMENT EXPENSES
HOME	$1,350	$300
TRANSPORTATION	$425	$250
FOOD/CLOTHING	$550	$350
PERSONAL	$450	$400
HEALTH	$50	$300
SUPPORT TO OTHERS	$250	$300
RECREATION/ENTERTAIN	$230	$700
TAXES	$900	$500
CONTRIBUTIONS/MISC	$75	$200
TOTALS =	$4,280	$3,300

$3,300 a month. If inflation increases at 3 percent per year, he'll need $6,909 a month to retire on in 25 years. But what if inflation averages 6 percent a year during that time? To maintain the same standard of living, he'll need $14,163 per month! If he continues to live 15 years past retirement age, he'll need more than $23,000 per month, or more than $250,000 per year.

Worksheet 16.2 essentially is a table which will allow you to calculate the monthly income needed at retirement, with inflation taken into consideration. The formula used to calculate this retirement monthly income is as follows:

(Today's Income) × (1 + Inflation rate)^Number of years to retirement

For example, ($3,300)*(1 + 4 percent)^25.

Be careful if you enter the formula by pointing the cursor to the appropriate cells. If you do, remember to go back using EDIT mode to add the parentheses around the variables. Don't forget to include the *1 +* Inflation Rate in your formula.

FINANCIAL INDEPENDENCE AT RETIREMENT

Financial experts see cost-of-living increases as

```
WORKSHEET  16.2:   INCOME NEEDED FOR RETIREMENT


MARGINS:   LEFT=5, RIGHT=75

COLUMNS:   GLOBAL=15, A=12

FORMAT:    COMMAS, NO DECIMALS

PRINTER:   COMPRESS=OFF

RUN:       ANNUALLY
```

RETINC   22-Oct-84

WORKSHEET 16.2:   INCOME NEEDED FOR RETIREMENT

RETIREMENT INCOME NEEDED A	INFLATION RATE B	YEARS TIL UNTIL RETIRTEMENT C	AMOUNT NEEDED PER MONTH A*(1+B)^C	AMOUNT NEEDED PER YEAR
$3,300	3.00%	25	$6,909	$82,914
$3,300	4.00%	25	$8,797	$105,567
$3,300	5.00%	25	$11,175	$134,100
$3,300	6.00%	25	$14,163	$169,958
$3,300	7.00%	25	$17,911	$214,926
$3,300	8.00%	25	$22,600	$271,200

the biggest threat to financial independence at retirement. If we assume a long-term inflation rate of just 7 percent, our costs today would double in 10 years.

The main message of this section is that advance planning is necessary for a secure retirement. Worksheet 16.3 will help you in planning how to attain financial independence at retirement. It lists all your assets and liabilities and their present worth. It assumes a growth rate for the assets until you retire, and allows you to decrease your liabilities at a certain percentage rate until retirement. It then calculates the future value of your assets and liabilities and calculates your net worth at retirement. Any or all of these figures can be changed at any time and the spreadsheet instantly recalculated.

In Worksheet 16.1 we took Mr. and Mrs. Somebody's total assets from their Personal Financial Statement (Worksheet 9.1) and combined that with the estimated return on investment information from Worksheet 12.1.

Then we designed a worksheet with a variable table, which allows us to enter in different assumptions for the various assets. There is no limit to the number of variables you can add to your table. You can have one variable for every asset, and this would allow you to start with a beginning asset dollar amount and have the variable be the amount you add to that asset each year.

In our worksheet, we used two assumptions and four annual contributions. The assumptions were: a financial goal of $1 million, and 25 years to retirement. The annual contributions were: savings ($1,000), IRA,KEOGH ($3,000), money market fund ($1,000), and purchase of company stock ($2,000).

The worksheet allows us to change these variables and also enter a separate growth rate for each asset. We therefore use our two key formulas in the worksheet: compounded growth rate and future value of an asset. An example of the formula for calculating the compounding value of an asset is as follows: Asset = $950, Percent growth = 5 percent, Number of years until retirement = 25:

$$(950)*(1.05)^{\wedge}25$$

The formula for computing the future value of the IRA and savings plan is as follows, with Annual Savings = $1,000, Rate of Return = 8 percent, Number of years = 25:

@FV(Annual Savings, Rate of Return, Number of Years)

CONSTRUCTING A RETIREMENT MODEL

Worksheet 16.4 is another example of using a

WORKSHEET 16.3:   PROJECTION OF NET WORTH AT RETIREMENT

MARGINS: LEFT=5, RIGHT=75

COLUMNS: GLOBAL=13, A=18

FORMAT: COMMAS, NO DECIMALS

PRINTER: COMPRESS=OFF

SORT BY: PERCENT GROWTH, DECENDING

RUN AT: YEAR END

```
WORKSHEET  16.3:   PROJECTION OF NET WORTH AT RETIREMENT
------------------------------------------------------------------
ASSUMPTIONS:
   FINANCIAL GOAL =               $1,000,000
   YEARS TIL RETIREMENT =                 25

ANNUAL CONTRIBUTIONS:
          SAVINGS =                   $1,000
          IRA/KEOGH =                 $3,000
          MONEY MARKET =              $1,000
          COMPANY STOCK =             $2,000
------------------------------------------------------------------
ASSETS              PRESENT        % GROWTH   RETIREMENT $
------------------------------------------------------------------
SAVINGS               6,000          8.00%        73,106
IRA/KEOGH             5,500         12.00%       400,002
MONEY MARKET          2,000          8.00%        73,106
COMPANY STOCK         6,500          9.00%       169,402
BONDS                 3,000          5.00%        10,159
REAL ESTATE         145,000          3.00%       303,598
PERSONAL             33,500          1.00%        42,961
------------------------------------------------------------------
TOTALS=            $201,500                   $1,072,334


LIABILITIES         PRESENT                   RETIREMENT $
------------------------------------------------------------------
CURR BILLS            1,950                              0
AUTO LOANS            5,000                              0
OTHER LOANS           5,000                              0
HOME MTG             30,000                              0
CABIN MTG            21,000                              0
TAXES                 3,000                              0
------------------------------------------------------------------
TOTALS=             $65,950                            $0


NET WORTH =        $135,550                   $1,072,334
                   ========                   ==========
```

variable table to estimate the growth of assets and investments. The four assumptions are: Present value of Assets ($58,000), Annual Rate of Return on those assets (12%), Annual tax-free savings ($2,000), Percent Tax Bracket (42%).

The worksheet calculates for each year the following values:

1. The beginning estimated cash value of the investments or assets.

2. The realized taxable gain, which is computed by multiplying the investment amount by the annual rate of return.

3. The tax amount paid on the gain, which is the realized taxable gain multiplied by the percent

WORKSHEET 16.4: ESTIMATING THE GROWTH OF ASSETS TO
RETIREMENT

MARGINS: LEFT=5, RIGHT=75

COLUMNS: GLOBAL=12, A=5

FORMAT: COMMAS, NO DECIMALS

PRINTER: COMPRESS=OFF

RUN AT: YEAR END

RETEST   22-Oct-84

WORKSHEET 16.4: ESTIMATING THE GROWTH OF ASSETS TO RETIREMENT

ASSUMPTIONS:

    PRESENT VALUE OF ASSETS (A) $58,000
    ANNUAL RATE OF RETURN (B)   8.00%
    ANNUAL TAX-FREE SAVINGS (C) $2,000
    PERCENT TAX BRACKET (D)   42.00%

YEAR	INVESTMENT CASH VALUE (E)	REALIZED TAXABLE GAIN (F=E*B)	LESS TAX (G=E*D)	TAX-FREE SAVINGS (H=H+C+I)	TAX-FREE INCOME (I=E*B)	INVESTMENTS SAVED/EARNED (E+F-G+H+I)
1	58,000	4,640	1,949	2,000	160	62,851
2	62,851	5,028	2,112	4,160	333	70,260
3	70,260	5,621	2,361	6,493	519	80,533
4	80,533	6,443	2,706	9,012	721	94,003
5	94,003	7,520	3,158	11,733	939	111,036
6	111,036	8,883	3,731	14,672	1,174	132,034
7	132,034	10,563	4,436	17,846	1,428	157,433
8	157,433	12,595	5,290	21,273	1,702	187,713
9	187,713	15,017	6,307	24,975	1,998	223,396
10	223,396	17,872	7,506	28,973	2,318	265,053
11	265,053	21,204	8,906	33,291	2,663	313,306
12	313,306	25,064	10,527	37,954	3,036	368,834
13	368,834	29,507	12,393	42,991	3,439	432,377
14	432,377	34,590	14,528	48,430	3,874	504,744
15	504,744	40,380	16,959	54,304	4,344	586,813
16	586,813	46,945	19,717	60,649	4,852	679,541
17	679,541	54,363	22,833	67,500	5,400	783,972
18	783,972	62,718	26,341	74,900	5,992	901,241
19	901,241	72,099	30,282	82,893	6,631	1,032,583
20	1,032,583	82,607	34,695	91,524	7,322	1,179,340
21	1,179,340	94,347	39,626	100,846	8,068	1,342,975
22	1,342,975	107,438	45,124	110,914	8,873	1,525,076
23	1,525,076	122,006	51,243	121,787	9,743	1,727,369
24	1,727,369	138,190	58,040	133,530	10,682	1,951,731
25	1,951,731	156,138	65,578	146,212	11,697	2,200,200

tax bracket.

4. The tax-free savings, which is the compounding of the annual savings contribution times the annual rate of return.

5. The actual tax-free income amount for that year.

6. The total investment amount, plus the after-tax amount saved and the tax-free amount earned.

There are additional assumptions which you can add to your variable table: for example, an annual stock investment amount, an optimistic and a pessimistic rate of return, etc. Even though the information is only tentative, each time you revise your original model you will be nearer to developing one that will be actuality.

You owe it to yourself to determine your retirement goals now. What you do now will not only affect your present way of life, it will assure a new way of living in retirement. Retirement should be culmination of a lifetime of work—a time to do what you want when you want to do it. It can and will be the time of your life - if you plan for it.

SECTION 6

INVESTMENTS

Portfolio Management

No matter what the size of your portfolio, keeping records is an important but time-consuming activity. The worksheets offered in this book will not tell you when to buy or sell a stock, but they will provide you with important time-saving tools which will help you manage your investments. These worksheets will store and display financial information accurately and completely and provide you with useful reports and analyses. Besides giving you a picture of each investment you won, these worksheets will give you a complete picture of your entire portfolio.

ORGANIZING YOUR INVESTMENTS

There are some phases of portfolio management that are best done manually by you, and others best done by a computer. Tracking investments like stocks and bonds on a daily basis when information changes quickly makes it impractical to key directly into a computer. If you want to track the daily stock market or commodities market, I recommend that you subscribe to a news service or purchase special computer software to aid you in this endeavor.

There are literally hundreds of software programs and dozens of on-line databases to choose from. For example, you can tap into the Dow Jones News/Retrieval Service and download onto your own disk the price and volume information about the stocks you are interested in tracking. Then with the Dow Jones Market Analyzer you can graph the highs and lows of your stocks.

The cost for using these on-line services can add up, of course. Rates can run from $6 to more than $100 an hour depending on the kind of service you have.

If you want to take the information and analyze it at your leisure, *Value Line Investment Survey* has an offering called "Value/Screen," which lets you store information from more than 1,650 stocks on a single disk. It is offered for an annual fee, which is tax-deductible if used in managing your investments.

A less expensive way is to do it manually.

There are many manual systems commercially available. One of the more popular ones is called *Securities and Income Records at a Glance*, Published by the Shaeffer-Eaton Division of Textron, Inc. You can find it in most stationery stores.

BUYING AND SELLING STOCKS AND BONDS

Although it is possible to track your stock portfolio manually, one frequently must compare annual yields based on current stock price in order to select the best investment opportunity. These calculations are time consuming. Now there is an easier way.

The next four worksheets in this chapter offer you a practical system of tracking your portfolio over a long period of time. Not having a good system of record keeping can be costly. Have you ever tried to reconstruct the price paid for stocks purchased over a number of years, in order to justify their cost for an IRS audit?

Worksheet 17.1 shows how you can track your stock investments. It will tell you what stocks you own, how much you paid for them, and how much you really make or lose after commissions. You will know instantly how much money your portfolio has gained or lost.

Begin by entering the stocks and bonds in your portfolio. For each security you simply input the name, purchase date, number of shares purchased, and the annual dividend/interest. Then add the unit cost and the broker's commission. Have the worksheet calculate the total dollars invested.

(# of Shares × Unit Cost) + Broker's Comm = Total Investment

When you sell some shares, enter the date of sale, number of shares sold, unit price, amount received, and broker's commission. Have the worksheet calculate Net Gain/Loss.

WORKSHEET 17.1: HISTORY OF SECURITIES BOUGHT AND SOLD

MARGINS: LEFT=2, RIGHT=132

COLUMNS: GLOBAL=10, A=12

FORMAT: COMMAS, TWO DECIMALS

PRINTER: COMPRESS=ON

SORT BY: PURCHASE DATE

RUN AT: AS NEEDED

STOCKS   22-Oct-84

WORKSHEET 17.1: HISTORY OF SECURITIES BOUGHT AND SOLD

| | A | B | C | D | E | F | G | H | I | J | K | L | M |
NAME OF SECURITY	PURCHASE DATE	DIVIDENDS INTEREST	NO. OF SHARES	UNIT COST	BROKER'S COMM	TOTAL INVEST	DATE OF SALE	NO. OF SHARES	UNIT PRICE	AMOUNT REC'D	BROKER'S COMM	NET GAIN/LOSS
NXXON	24-May-79	18.43	100	33.125	47.14	3,359.64	22-Oct-84	100	40.750	4,075.00	51.34	$682.45
BIG COPR	24-Oct-79	3.80	100	55.250	98.43	5,623.43						
DYNAMIC CO	11-Feb-80	0.44	200	22.50	76.44	4,576.44	12-Dec-83	200	19.125	3,825.00	75.00	($826.00)
STG MOTORS	11-Jun-80	7.71	200	36.50	165.32	7,465.32	12-Dec-83	200	69.125	13,825.00	185.00	$6,182.39
GOBIL OIL	27-Aug-82	2.20	100	25.13	40.65	2,512.50						
STEARS	27-Sep-83	0.32	300	16.00	88.31	4,800.00						
						28,337.33				21,725.00		6,038.83

(# of shares × Unit Price) – Broker's Comm = Net Gain/Loss

In addition to the stock information shown in Worksheet 17.1, you might add the stock ticker symbol, dividend rate, present yield, income from the security, and the percent of the total portfolio represented by each security.

There are also several ways you can print this report. You can list your investments alphabetically by name, by industry group, in descending sequence of present market value, or by income generated. Some of these options are incorporated in later reports.

HOW TO ANALYZE YOUR INVESTMENTS

Worksheet 17.2 helps you to analyze the total return on all your investments. The first thing you do is enter the investment name, date of purchase, number of units, and cost per share. The worksheet calculates the total cost. The worksheet then allows

WORKSHEET 17.2:   ANALYSIS OF CURRENT INVESTMENTS

MARGINS: LEFT=3, RIGHT=132

COLUMNS: GLOBAL=10

FORMAT: COMMAS, TWO DECIMALS

PRINTER: COMPRESS=ON

SORT BY: DATE OF PURCHASE

RUN: AS NEEDED

STRETURN   22-Oct-84

WORKSHEET 17.2: ANALYSIS OF CURRENT INVESTMENTS   -   BY DATE OF PURCHASE

INVESTMENT	DATE PURCHASED	NO. OF SHARES	COST PER SHARE	TOTAL COST	TODAY'S PRICE	TODAY'S VALUE	TOTAL GAIN/LOSS	PERCENT RETURN	ANNUALIZED RETURN
COMPUCORP	24-Oct-79	50	25.25	1,262.50	29.50	1,475.00	212.50	16.83%	3.32%
STOCK FUND	25-Jan-81	55	22.78	1,252.90	36.78	2,022.90	770.00	61.46%	16.20%
OIL/GAS	30-Jan-82	10	500.00	5,000.00	450.00	4,500.00	(500.00)	-10.00%	-3.61%
MOBIL OIL	27-Aug-82	100	25.13	2,513.00	26.13	2,612.50	99.50	3.96%	1.81%
SMC STOCK	30-Dec-83	50	80.07	4,003.50	88.00	4,400.00	396.50	9.90%	12.00%
MUTUAL FD	18-Jan-84	600	12.23	7,338.00	14.01	8,406.00	1,068.00	14.55%	18.85%
				$21,369.90		$23,416.40	$2,047	16.12%	8.09%

the entry of today's current price and calculates today's total value by multiplying today's price by the number of shares owned. It also computes any gain or loss for each investment (Today's Value - Total Cost).

The percent return is computed by dividing total gain or loss by total cost. These figures are then summed at the bottom of the report. The average percent return is computed using the Lotus 1-2-3 @AVG function, e.g.:

@AVG(I10 . . . I20)

The annualized return formula is shown on the worksheet and is calculated as follows:

Percent Return /((Today's Date - Date of Purchase) / 365 days)

This worksheet can be sorted several ways: by date of purchase, investment, total value, or percent return. You also can assign your ranking value to each asset and keep tabs on them that way.

This report should be run whenever you buy or sell an investment and at the end of each month.

MULTIPLE STOCK PURCHASES

Quite often investors have the opportunity to purchase their companies' stock through an employees' stock purchase plan. The advantages are that you usually can purchase the stock at a discount and that purchases are made through regular payroll deductions, often without any commission charge. The disadvantage is that it is difficult to keep track of when you bought the stock and at what price.

Worksheet 17.3A helps you organize and analyze the yield on a stock that you are purchasing repeatedly. The top of the worksheet shows the stock price as of today's date and the annual dividend. The body of the report shows the date the stock was purchased, the number of shares, and the purchase price. The worksheet calculates the total cost (#Shares × unit cost), then calculates the dividend yield based on the unit cost, for example:

Yield = (Dividend Amount * 4) / Unit Cost

Total return takes into consideration the number of quarters and the amount of dividend each stock earned. This calculation is done at column AA18 through column AA45. The formula for computing the dividend amount earned is as follows:

$$@INT((+\$G\$-A18/90)*\$F\$12$$

(@TODAY – Purchase Date/#Qtrs) *Qtr Dividend Amount

Total return adds the dividend amount earned on each share to today's price and subtracts unit cost and multiplies this by the number of shares. For example, the January 15, 1983, total return is computed as follows:

$$+B18 * (AA18+\$F\$11) - D18$$

#Shares * (Dividends Earned + Today's Price) – Unit Cost

The Percent Return is computed by dividing the total return by the total cost.

Total Return / Total Cost = Percent Total

These figures are calculated for each share purchased and totaled at the bottom. A horizontal window at the bottom of the worksheet makes it easy to see the effects of a price fluctuation or a change in the dividend rate. You also can compute the high and low purchase cost of the stock for the past year using the @MIN and @MAX functions.

There are actually several uses for Worksheet 17.1. It can help you track the price performance of a stock over a period of time. You can compare past price trends with current prices to estimate the future performance of the stock.

Worksheet 17.3B has been expanded to allow you to enter information about the sale of the stock, such as date sold, number of shares sold, unit price, amount received, brokers commissions, and net gain or loss.

WORKSHEET 17.3AB: ANALYSIS OF MONTHLY STOCK PURCHASES

MARGINS: LEFT=3, RIGHT=85

COLUMNS: GLOBAL=12, B=6

FORMAT: COMMAS, DECIMALS

PRINTER: COMPRESS=OFF

SORT BY: DATE OF PURCHASE

RUN AT: AS NEEDED

WORKSHEET 17.3A: ANALYSIS OF MONTHLY STOCK PURCHASE

JAMES T. SOMEBODY

MONTHLY STOCK PURCHASE PLAN
SALES MARKETING CORPORATION (SMC)

PRICE AS OF 15-Oct-84 EQUALS $78.00
QUARTERLY DIVIDEND EQUALS $0.70

DATE OF PURCHASE	#SHRS	UNIT COST	TOTAL COST	TODAY'S VALUE	YIELD ON COST	TOTAL RETURN	PERCENT RETURN
15-Jan-83	3	60.31	180.93	234.00	4.64%	67.77	37.46%
21-Jan-83	1	61.30	61.30	78.00	4.57%	21.60	35.24%
31-Jan-83	2	63.15	126.30	156.00	4.43%	38.10	30.17%
15-Feb-83	2	64.69	129.38	156.00	4.33%	35.02	27.07%
28-Feb-83	2	84.79	169.58	156.00	3.30%	(5.18)	-3.05%
15-Mar-83	2	85.38	170.76	156.00	3.28%	(6.36)	-3.72%
31-Mar-83	2	75.38	150.76	156.00	3.71%	13.64	9.05%
31-Mar-83	2	87.77	175.54	156.00	3.19%	(11.14)	-6.35%
15-Apr-83	2	73.56	147.12	156.00	3.81%	17.28	11.75%
29-Apr-83	1	79.30	79.30	78.00	3.53%	2.20	2.77%
13-May-83	2	78.71	157.42	156.00	3.56%	5.58	3.54%
15-May-83	1	74.13	74.13	78.00	3.78%	7.37	9.94%
31-May-83	2	64.83	129.66	156.00	4.32%	33.34	25.71%
15-Jun-83	2	64.63	129.26	156.00	4.33%	33.74	26.10%
30-Jun-83	1	62.32	62.32	78.00	4.49%	19.18	30.78%
15-Jul-83	2	63.54	127.08	156.00	4.41%	35.92	28.27%
29-Jul-83	2	62.64	125.28	156.00	4.47%	36.32	28.99%
15-May-83	2	62.27	124.54	156.00	4.50%	38.46	30.88%
31-Aug-83	1	60.52	60.52	78.00	4.63%	20.28	33.51%
15-Sep-83	2	63.97	127.94	156.00	4.38%	33.66	26.31%
27-Sep-83	2	72.00	144.00	156.00	3.89%	17.60	12.22%
30-Sep-83	2	78.22	156.44	156.00	3.58%	5.16	3.30%
14-Oct-83	1	72.42	72.42	78.00	3.87%	8.38	11.57%
31-Oct-83	2	78.70	157.40	156.00	3.56%	2.80	1.78%
15-Nov-83	2	76.95	153.90	156.00	3.64%	6.30	4.09%
30-Nov-83	2	81.90	163.80	156.00	3.42%	(3.60)	-2.20%
15-Dec-83	1	72.48	72.48	78.00	3.86%	7.62	10.51%
30-Dec-83	2	74.29	148.58	156.00	3.77%	11.62	7.82%
	50	$71.33	$3,429.56	$3,744.00	3.98%	$481.04	14.03%

MINIMUM = $60.31   MAXIMUM = $87.77

JAMES T. SOMEBODY CAN BORROW ON SMC STOCK PLAN
   75.00% OF TODAY'S TOTAL VALUE $3,744.00 i.e., $2,808.00
                                                    ==========

WORKSHEET 17.3B: ANALYSIS OF MONTHLY STOCK PURCHASE

JAMES T. SOMEBODY

MONTHLY STOCK PURCHASE PLAN
SALES MARKETING CORPORATION (SMC)

PRICE AS OF 22-Oct-84 EQUALS $78.00
QUARTERLY DIVIDEND EQUALS $0.70

DATE OF PURCHASE	#SHRS	UNIT COST	TOTAL COST	TODAY'S VALUE	YIELD ON COST	TOTAL RETURN	PERCENT RETURN	DATE SOLD	#SHRS	UNIT PRICE	AMOUNT REC'D	SELLING COST	NET GAIN/LOSS
15-Jan-83	3	60.31	180.93	234.00	4.64%	67.77	37.46%						
21-Jan-83	1	61.30	61.30	78.00	4.57%	21.60	35.24%						
31-Jan-83	2	63.15	126.30	156.00	4.43%	39.50	31.27%						
15-Feb-83	2	64.69	129.38	156.00	4.33%	35.02	27.07%						
28-Feb-83	2	84.79	169.58	156.00	3.30%	(5.18)	-3.05%						
15-Mar-83	2	85.38	170.76	156.00	3.28%	(6.36)	-3.72%						
31-Mar-83	2	75.38	150.76	156.00	3.71%	13.64	9.05%						
31-Mar-83	2	87.77	175.54	156.00	3.19%	(11.14)	-6.35%						
15-Apr-83	2	73.56	147.12	156.00	3.81%	17.28	11.75%						
29-Apr-83	1	79.30	79.30	78.00	3.53%	2.90	3.66%						
13-May-83	2	78.71	157.42	156.00	3.56%	5.58	3.54%						
15-May-83	1	74.13	74.13	78.00	3.78%	7.37	9.94%						
31-May-83	2	64.83	129.66	156.00	4.32%	33.34	25.71%						
15-Jun-83	2	64.63	129.26	156.00	4.33%	33.74	26.10%						
30-Jun-83	1	62.32	62.32	78.00	4.49%	19.18	30.78%						
15-Jul-83	2	63.54	127.08	156.00	4.41%	35.92	28.27%						
29-Jul-83	2	62.64	125.28	156.00	4.47%	37.72	30.11%						
15-May-83	2	62.27	124.54	156.00	4.50%	38.46	30.88%						
31-Aug-83	1	60.52	60.52	78.00	4.63%	20.28	33.51%						
15-Sep-83	2	63.97	127.94	156.00	4.38%	33.66	26.31%						
27-Sep-83	2	72.00	144.00	156.00	3.89%	17.60	12.22%						
30-Sep-83	2	78.22	156.44	156.00	3.58%	5.16	3.30%						
14-Oct-83	1	72.42	72.42	78.00	3.87%	8.38	11.57%						
31-Oct-83	2	78.70	157.40	156.00	3.56%	2.80	1.78%						
15-Nov-83	2	76.95	153.90	156.00	3.64%	6.30	4.09%						
30-Nov-83	2	81.90	163.80	156.00	3.42%	(3.60)	-2.20%						
15-Dec-83	1	72.48	72.48	78.00	3.86%	7.62	10.51%						
30-Dec-83	2	74.29	148.58	156.00	3.77%	11.62	7.82%						

| | 50 | 71.33 | 3,429.56 | 3,744.00 | 3.98% | 484.54 | 14.13% | | | | | | |

JAMES T. SOMEBODY CAN BORROW ON SMC STOCK PLAN

75.00% OF TODAY'S TOTAL VALUE $3,744.00 i.e., $2,808.00
                                               =========

PORTFOLIO PROFIT AND LOSS

Worksheet 17.4 will assist you in preparing your Federal Income Tax Form 1040 and Schedule D, Capital Gains and Losses.

Examples of property to be reported on this worksheet are gains and losses on stock, bonds and similar investments, and gains (but not losses) on personal assets such as home jewelry.

With this worksheet, you can double-check all of your broker's paperwork and end-of-year statements, as well as have a running total of your investment portfolio that you can run and analyze at any time.

RECORDING DIVIDENDS AND INTEREST

Income stocks are relatively easy to select as compared to growth stocks. You want stocks that not only pay good dividends, but also have a good record of increasing their dividends.

Income stocks usually pay out 65-75 percent of their net earnings in cash dividends. Once a regular dividend rate has been established, it is unlikely that it will be reduced because of poor earnings in a single year.

The dividend amount also is referred to as the dividend yield. This can be calculated by dividing the annual dividend by the price of the stock. The

---

```
WORKSHEET 17.4:   PORTFOLIO PROFIT AND LOSS


    MARGINS:   LEFT=2, RIGHT=85

    COLUMNS:   GLOBAL =10,  A=12,  B=7,  C=9

    COLUMNS:   DOLLARS & CENTS

    PRINTER:   COMPRESS=OFF

    RUN:       AS NEEDED
```

STGAIN   22-Oct-84

WORKSHEET 17.4:   PORTFOLIO PROFIT AND LOSS

DESCRIPTION	UNITS	DATE ACQUIRED	DATE SOLD	GROSS SALES $	COST AND EXP OF SALE	GAIN/LOSS
XYZ CORP	300	13-Apr-83	15-Apr-83	4,950.00	2,520.12	2,429.88
Century S&L	100	03-Jun-82	01-May-83	3,525.00	4,663.78	(1,138.78)
Micro Elect	400	03-Jun-82	11-Jun-83	1,300.00	2,344.31	(1,044.31)
Modern Tech	500	03-Jun-82	01-Jul-83	125.00	409.90	(284.90)
Gen Hosp Co	200	03-Jun-82	12-Aug-83	6,650.00	3,088.53	3,561.47
New CompSevr	1000	03-Jun-82	31-Aug-83	1,250.00	1,797.65	(547.65)
				17,800.00	14,824.29	2,975.71

dividend helps to keep up the total yield of a stock. For example, take Mr. Somebody's SMC Corporation stock, selling at $78, and paying an annual dividend of $2.80 a share, a 4 percent dividend yield. Say the stock drops to $58, but dividends remain unchanged. At that price, the stock yields 5 percent, which may cause some investors to buy the stock. In this way, the dividend helps keep the price from falling too far.

Many stocks offer dividend reinvestment plans (DRP). These companies give you the option of automatically reinvesting your quarterly dividends in additional shares of stock. Most DRP's grant shareholders direct cash investment privileges—a good way to reduce or eliminate brokerage commissions and put more of your money to work. Some companies also offer a discount on shares purchased through a dividend reinvestment plan.

Worksheet 17.5 will help you track your dividend income. You should have one dividend worksheet for each stock you own, and perhaps a summary worksheet. Our worksheet is an example of Mr. Somebody's dividend reinvestment plan with SMC Corporation over the past 3 1/2 years. It shows dividend date, number of shares held, dividend rate per share, dividend amount, and the cumulative amount to date.

HOW WELL IS YOUR FUND DOING?

Sometimes it is difficult for an investor to determine the total return on a mutual stock fund. Newspapers list only the daily net asset value (NAV) of a fund. This represents the fund's total assets divided by the number of fund shares outstanding.

Taken by themselves, however, these prices don't tell you how well or how poorly the fund has been performing. Suppose, for instance, that the NAV shows virtually no change for some extended period, say a year. Does this mean that the fund is not making money? Not at all. The fund might have distributed dividends and capital gains during that period.

You can't get the true measure of a fund's performance, therefore, unless you take dividends and capital gains payments into account. Essentially, that's what funds do when they issue their periodic reports to shareholders. But these reports don't necessarily cover the period in which you're interested. You can use the next worksheet to compute your fund's performance.

Doing your own total-return worksheet requires some work. You need to know the dates and amounts of all payouts during the period you are evaluating. You can get this information from the

```
WORKSHEET 17.5:   DIVIDEND RECORD


MARGINS:   LEFT=5, RIGHT=75


COLUMNS:   GLOBAL=12

FORMAT:    DOLLARS AND CENTS

PRINTER:   COMPRESS=OFF

RUN:       QUARTERLY
```

WORKSHEET 17.5: DIVIDEND RECORD

COMPANY: SMC CORPORATION

DIVIDEND DATE	NO. OF SHARES	RATE PER SHARE	DIVIDEND AMOUNT	CUMMULATIVE TO-DATE
31-Mar-80	125	0.55	68.75	68.75
30-Jun-80	131	0.55	72.05	140.80
30-Sep-80	137	0.55	75.35	216.15
31-Dec-80	143	0.55	78.65	294.80
			$294.80	
31-Mar-81	149	0.60	89.40	384.20
30-Jun-81	155	0.60	93.00	477.20
30-Sep-81	161	0.60	96.60	573.80
31-Dec-81	168	0.60	100.80	674.60
			$379.80	
31-Mar-82	175	0.65	113.75	788.35
30-Jun-82	183	0.65	118.95	907.30
30-Sep-82	190	0.65	123.50	1,030.80
31-Dec-82	197	0.65	128.05	1,158.85
			$484.25	
31-Mar-83	204	0.65	132.60	1,291.45
30-Jun-83	214	0.70	149.80	1,441.25
30-Sep-83	220	0.70	154.00	1,595.25
31-Dec-83	227	0.70	158.90	1,754.15
			$595.30	
31-Mar-84	234	0.70	163.80	1,917.95
30-Jun-84	241	0.70	168.70	2,086.65
			$332.50	

---

cumulative statement which is mailed out once a year, or whenever there is a transaction in your account.

Worksheet 17.6 shows how the total return is computed for the GOGO Mutual Stock Fund. It shows transaction date, amount bought or sold, share cost, number of shares, income and capital gains, total shares owned, and value of shares held.

The value of shares owned is computed by multiplying total shares owned by today's net asset value. The percent return is computed by dividing the unrealized gain or loss by the total amount invested. The worksheet assumes that all dividends and capital gains are reinvested in the fund.

```
              WORKSHEET  17.6:  RECORD OF MUTUAL STOCK FUND



              MARGINS:  LEFT=0, RIGHT=95

              COLUMNS:  GLOBAL=10, B=12, C=8, E=8, F=8

              FORMAT:   DOLLARS AND CENTS

              PRINTER:  COMPRESS=OFF

              RUN:      AS NEEDED
```

```
FUND                                                          22-Oct-84

WORKSHEET  17.6:  RECORD OF MUTUAL STOCK FUND
-----------------------------------------------------------------------

                    GOGO MUTUAL STOCK FUND

         SHARE PRICE AS OF    22-Oct-84 EQUALS              $14.20

         TOTAL NUMBER OF SHARES OWNED =                     291.555

         TODAY'S NET ASSET VALUE OF SHARES OWNED =       $4,140.07
         TOTAL AMOUNT INVESTED EQUALS =                  $3,090.03
                                                         -----------
         UNREALIZED GAIN/LOSS =                          $1,050.04

         PERCENT RETURN =                                  33.98%
```

TRADE DATE	TRANSACTION AMOUNT BUY/SELL	SHARE COST	NUMBER OF SHARES	INCOME AMOUNT	CAPITAL GAINS	TOTAL SHARES OWNED	VALUE OF SHARES HELD
20-Dec-80	$1,000.00	10.560	94.697			94.697	$1,000.00
29-Dec-80		10.510	1.441	15.15		96.138	$1,010.42
29-Dec-80		10.510	2.072		21.78	98.211	$1,032.20
26-Jan-81	$1,436.03	11.610	123.689			221.900	$2,576.26
12-Dec-81		12.030	4.635	55.76		226.535	$2,725.21
12-Dec-81		12.030	9.052		108.90	235.587	$2,834.11
20-Jan-82	($1,346.00)	13.460	-100.000			135.587	$1,825.00
14-Dec-82		13.480	0.915	12.33		136.502	$1,840.05
14-Dec-82		13.480	4.295		57.89	140.796	$1,897.94
16-Jan-83	$1,000.00	14.830	67.431			208.227	$3,088.01
15-Dec-83		15.070	1.244	18.74		209.471	$3,156.73
04-Dec-83		15.070	5.279		79.55	214.750	$3,236.28
11-Feb-84	$1,000.00	13.020	76.805			291.555	$3,796.04
	$3,090.03			$101.98	$268.12		

Investment Planning

Leverage means that you borrow money and invest it together with your own in order to get a higher return on your money.

THE EFFECT OF LEVERAGE

The decision to borrow money will ultimately rest on your assessment of the potential return on the investment. If you are confident that this return will exceed the cost of money, then by all means "leverage up." If you are not sure of the return, the more conservative strategy would be to use more of your own money.

Worksheet 18.1 illustrates the effects of leverage. It assumes you want to buy $10,000 worth of stock upon which you expect to earn 20 percent next year. If your current tax rate is 40 percent, how should you buy this stock—pay for it all now or buy it on margin and borrow from your broker at 15 percent interest?

The worksheet shows a return on equity of 12 percent when the stock is purchased outright, and a 16.5 percent return when it is purchased on margin. Return on equity is arrived at by dividing after-tax income by the original amount of the investment.

Remember, however, that leverage is a two-edged sword. It's great if the value of the investment goes up, but it also magnifies losses. Suppose that $10,000 investment declined in value to $8,000. Now you've got a 25 percent loss on assets, but a 50 percent loss on your investment. In other words, small changes in rate of return will result in dramatic changes to return on equity.

Worksheet 18.1 can show you what happens if you guess wrong on the stock. If you substitute a rate of return of 12 percent, you find that borrowing the funds does not make sense in this case. A rule of thumb: if the odds of winning or losing are even, leverage is a bad idea. The interest you pay tilts the balance against you.

LEVERAGE: THE CORNERSTONE OF INVESTING

One of the cornerstones of creative financial

WORKSHEET 18.1: THE EFFECTS OF LEVERAGE

MARGINS: LEFT=3, RIGHT=85

COLUMNS: GLOBAL=20, A=25

FORMAT: COMMAS, NO DECIMALS

PRINTER: COMPRESS OFF

RUN: AS NEEDED

WORKSHEET 18.1:   THE EFFECTS OF LEVERAGE

	OUTRIGHT PURCHASE 100% EQUITY	MARGIN PURCHASE 60% DEBT; 40% EQUITY
MARGIN AMOUNT BORROWED	$0	$6,000
YOUR OWN MONEY	$10,000	$4,000
TOTAL AMOUNT INVESTED	$10,000	$10,000
RETURN ON INVESTMENT	20.00%	20.00%
INCOME FROM INVESTMENT	$2,000	$2,000
INTEREST EXPENSE	0	$900
TAXABLE INCOME	$2,000	$1,100
TAXES @ 40%	$800	$440
AFTER TAX INCOME	$1,200	$660
RETURN ON EQUITY =	$1,200/$20,000=	$660/$4000=
	12.00%	16.50%

---

planning is the intelligent use of leverage. Worksheet 18.2 is one of the most significant time savers of the whole book. It calculates the effect of leverage on potential investments.

When interest rates are reasonable and stable, this report may be used to evaluate the merits of refinancing real estate to free dormant equity for a more creative investment. The example that follows will illustrate this point.

In 1976, Mr. and Mrs. Somebody paid $55,000 for their house in Anytown, USA. By 1984, the house was worth two times its purchase price, and with only $50,00 left on the mortgage, the Somebody's equity amounted to more than $60,000.

Now Mr. and Mrs. Somebody have the opportunity to take part in an investment which they hope will give them a 20 percent return over the next 15 years. The question is, how should they participate in the investment? They have two alternatives:

1. Tap the equity in their home with a 15 year, 14.5 percent second mortgage. The annual cost would be $4,172.

2. Save the $4,172 per year and invest the funds in the proposed investment each year over the next 15 years.

Which alternative is best? Our example allows a full comparison of either remaining with the status quo or applying leverage to your investment plans.

Both alternatives appear to have the same cost per year ($4,172). Both end up with about the same amount of invested capital, roughly $300,000. However, when looked at from the after-tax perspective, the equity loan alternative is clearly the winner.

In the case of the savings alternative, our couple, Mr. and Mrs. Somebody, would have invested $62,580 after-tax dollars to return $300,530, a 480 percent return on investment, or about 32 percent per year for 15 years.

With the equity loan example, our couple would

have invested only $37,545 in after-tax dollars to return $320,980, an 855 percent return, or about 57 percent per year for 15 years. That's fully 78 percent better than the savings alternative.

If you've owned a home for at least a few years, you're probably living in an asset that has appreciated handsomely. The equity in your home can be a tempting source of cash. But there are dangers in mortgaging your house to the hilt. Just because you have equity doesn't mean that you can afford the loan. Make sure you have the monthly income to make the monthly payments. If you invest in equity and rely on income from that investment to pay off the mortgage, the risks are especially grave. To cover your costs, the return has to exceed the mortgage rate.

CONSTRUCTING THE LEVERAGE MODEL

You can easily calculate the annual mortgage payment for any given principal by using Lotus 1-2-3's @PMT function. The format of this function is:

@PMT(Principal Amount, Interest Rate, Number of Years)

The annual mortgage payments at the top of Worksheet 18.2 were computed using the @PMT function, i.e.:

@PMT(55,000,.125,30)

@PMT(25,000,.145,15)

In the investment alternatives section, Column A is the cumulative investment total over the 15-year period. We start with the borrowed $25,000 and each year we add to it the 20 percent return. Column B shows us exactly how much the return actually was for each year. Column C represents our actual after-tax return (i.e., 60 percent of Column B since we assume a 40 percent tax bracket for Mr. Somebody). Column D is the after-tax percent return on our investment (i.e., $3,000/$2,503 = 119.86 percent).

In the Savings section, Column F shows us the cumulative savings over 15 years. Column G is the before-tax 20 percent return on our savings in Column F. The after-tax return in Column H is calculated by multiplying our return by our tax bracket of 40 percent (i.e., 60 percent of column G). The after-tax percent return in column I is computed by dividing the after-tax return by the after-tax costs. In year No. 1, for example, $501/$4,172 = 12.00 percent.

HOW MUCH DEBT CAN YOU HANDLE?

Borrowing can provide a most convenient way of meeting goals. Certainly with regard to housing, transportation, and such other major items as college tuition, borrowing allows you to accomplish what otherwise may take many years of ac-

---

WORKSHEET 18.2: LEVERAGE CASH FLOW ANALYSIS

MARGINS: LEFT=10, RIGHT=132

COLUMNS: GLOBAL=10

FORMAT: COMMAS, NO DECIMALS

PRINTER: COMPRESS=ON

RUN: AS NEEDED

WORKSHEET 18.2: LEVERAGE CASH FLOW ANALYSIS

ASSUMPTIONS:
- %BORROW $25,000 @ 12.5% FOR 15 YEARS - INVESTMENT PAYS 20%
- %OR, SAVE $4,172 A YEAR FOR 15 YEARS   - INVESTMENT PAYS 20%
- %40% TAX BRACKET

%INVESTMENT ALTERNATIVES%

1. TAKE OUT $25,000 HOME EQUITY LOAN | 2. SAVE $4,172 A YEAR FOR 15 YEARS

| | ANNUAL BEFORE TAX COST = | $4,172 | | | | ANNUAL BEFORE TAX COST = | $4,172 | | |
| | ANNUAL AFTER TAX COST = | $2,503 | | | | ANNUAL AFTER TAX COST = | $4,172 | | |

| YEAR | BORROW $25,000 | 20% RETURN | AFTER TAX RETURN | AFTER TAX PERCENT | YEAR | SAVE $4,172 | 20% RETURN | AFTER TAX RETURN | AFTER TAX PERCENT |
A	B	C	D	E	F	G	H	I	J
1	25,000	5,000	3,000	119.86%	1	4172	834	501	12.00%
2	30,000	6,000	3,600	143.83%	2	9,178	1,836	1,101	13.20%
3	36,000	7,200	4,320	172.59%	3	15,186	3,037	1,822	14.56%
4	43,200	8,640	5,184	207.11%	4	22,395	4,479	2,687	16.10%
5	51,840	10,368	6,221	248.53%	5	31,046	6,209	3,726	17.86%
6	62,208	12,442	7,465	298.24%	6	41,428	8,286	4,971	19.86%
7	74,650	14,930	8,958	357.89%	7	53,885	10,777	6,466	22.14%
8	89,580	17,916	10,750	429.47%	8	68,834	13,767	8,260	24.75%
9	107,495	21,499	12,899	515.36%	9	86,773	17,355	10,413	27.73%
10	128,995	25,799	15,479	618.43%	10	108,300	21,660	12,996	31.15%
11	154,793	30,959	18,575	742.12%	11	134,132	26,826	16,096	35.07%
12	185,752	37,150	22,290	890.54%	12	165,130	33,026	19,816	39.58%
13	222,903	44,581	26,748	1068.65%	13	202,328	40,466	24,279	44.77%
14	267,483	53,497	32,098	1282.38%	14	246,965	49,393	29,636	50.74%
15	320,980	64,196	38,518	1538.86%	15	300,530	60,106	36,064	57.63%

cumulating. Prudent borrowing can enhance your current, and continuing lifestyle. Imprudent borrowing can devastate your future lifestyle.

There is no one formula you can use to calculate total debt limits for yourself. Commercial lenders generally agree that when a firm's debts (liabilities) become equal to or greater than its equity (net worth), it is time to stop lending it money. You might use this debt/equity ratio as an upper limit on your borrowing. It should be measured exclusive of the value of your home and its mortgage.

Another way to measure your debt limit is to consider your ability to cover your debt payments out of your disposable income. If no more than 20 percent of your disposable income is used to make installment debt payments (exclusive of home mortgage), you probably will avoid misuse of debt.

Mr. and Mrs. Somebody generally agree that borrowing money is most effective when it is used to purchase assets. They also think that they should borrow money only at rates lower than they can achieve on their investment portfolio. The next two worksheets use information from previous chapters to calculate how leverage would affect the before and after-tax situation of the Somebody's future earnings. You can use these worksheets to make different comparisons of different strategies for tax purposes.

Begin by retrieving Worksheet 13.3 and changing the title and heading information to match those shown in Worksheet 18.3. This current model shows a 10 percent increase in all categories of income and most categories of deductions over the next three years. To be fair, we double the Somebodys' IRA/Keogh contribution from $2,000 to $4,000.

We use the 1984 Federal Tax Tables to estimate the federal tax for the years 1985, 1986 and 1987. State tax is assumed to be 20 percent of federal tax.

As you can see from the example, the Somebodys' taxable income rises dramatically over the next three years, and so do their taxes and tax bracket. Their total taxes paid almost double in the three-year period, from $8,116 to $12,905. Their tax bracket rose from 39.6 percent to 45.6 percent.

Next we'll look at ways to use leverage to reduce that tax liability.

HOW LEVERAGE AFFECTS CASH FLOW

In Worksheet 18.4 we will focus on reducing one item in the Somebodys' federal tax return: property income. We assume that the Somebodys have decided to purchase one tax shelter or buy one income property each year for the next three years. This has the effect of doubling the property income write-off each year from 1983 to 1986. This is the only change in their tax forecast.

As we can see in our example, by doubling the

WORKSHEET 18.3:   CASH FLOW BEFORE IMPLEMENTATION

MARGINS: LEFT=5, RIGHT=85

COLUMNS: GLOBAL=10, A=25

FORMAT: COMMAS, NO DECIMALS

PRINTER: COMPRESS=OFF

RUN AT: AS NEEDED

WORKSHEET 18.3   CASH FLOW BEFORE IMPLEMENTATION

GROSS INCOME	ACTUAL 1983	ESTIMATED 1984	1985	1986
Salary	31,000	34,100	37,510	41,261
Interest	300	330	363	399
Dividend	400	440	484	532
State tax refund	412	453	499	548
Business income	15,000	16,500	18,150	19,965
Property income	(1,592)	(1,751)	(1,926)	(2,119)
Capital gains	2,180	2,398	2,638	2,902
TOTAL INCOME	47,700	52,470	57,717	63,489
DEDUCTIONS				
Move expenses	0	0	0	0
Business expense	2,063	2,200	2,200	2,200
IRA/KEOGH	2,000	4,000	4,000	4,000
ADJUSTED GROSS	43,637	46,270	51,517	57,289
Medical expenses	147	162	178	196
State sales tax	1,099	1,209	1,330	1,463
Interest expense	5,108	5,200	5,200	5,200
Charity	385	424	466	512
Misc deductions	701	771	848	933
Zero tax bracket	(3,400)	(3,400)	(3,400)	(3,400)
Exemptions x 1000	4,000	4,000	4,000	4,000
TAXABLE INCOME	35,597	37,905	42,895	48,385
Total tax	6,405	7,167	8,813	10,754
Tax credit	0	0	0	0
TAXES: FEDERAL =	$6,763	$7,167	$8,813	$10,754
STATE =	$1,353	$1,433	$1,763	$2,151
TOTAL TAXES =	**$8,116**	**$8,600**	**$10,576**	**$12,905**
TAXES/INCOME =	17.01%	16.39%	18.32%	20.33%
TAX BRACKET:				
FEDERAL =	33.00%	33.00%	33.00%	38.00%
STATE =	6.60%	6.60%	6.60%	7.60%
TOTAL =	**39.60%**	**39.60%**	**39.60%**	**45.60%**

WORKSHEET 18.4: CASH FLOW AFTER IMPLEMENTATION

MARGINS: LEFT=5, RIGHT=85

COLUMNS: GLOBAL=10, A=25

FORMAT: COMMAS, NO DECIMALS

PRINTER: COMPRESS=OFF

RUN: AS NEEDED

AFTER   22-Oct-84

WORKSHEET 18.4: CASH FLOW AFTER IMPLEMENTATION

GROSS INCOME	ACTUAL		ESTIMATED	
	1983	1984	1985	1986
Salary	31,000	34,100	37,510	41,261
Interest	300	330	363	399
Dividend	400	440	484	532
State tax refund	412	453	499	548
Business income	15,000	16,500	18,150	19,965
Property income	(1,592)	(3,184)	(6,368)	(12,736)
Capital gains	2,180	2,398	2,638	2,902
TOTAL INCOME	47,700	51,037	53,275	52,872
DEDUCTIONS				
Move expenses	0	0	0	0
Business expense	2,063	2,200	2,200	2,200
IRA/KEOGH	2,000	4,000	4,000	4,000
ADJUSTED GROSS	43,637	44,837	47,075	46,672
Medical expenses	147	162	178	196
State sales tax	1,099	1,209	1,330	1,463
Interest expense	5,108	5,200	5,200	5,200
Charity	385	424	466	512
Misc deductions	701	771	848	933
Zero tax bracket	(3,400)	(3,400)	(3,400)	(3,400)
Exemptions x 1000	4,000	4,000	4,000	4,000
TAXABLE INCOME	35,597	36,472	38,454	37,768
Total tax	6,405	6,694	7,348	7,121
Tax credit	0	0	0	0
TAXES: FEDERAL =	$6,763	$6,694	$7,348	$7,121
STATE =	$1,353	$1,339	$1,470	$1,424
TOTAL TAXES =	$8,116	$8,033	$8,818	$8,545
TAXES/INCOME =	17.01%	15.74%	16.55%	16.16%
TAX BRACKET:				
FEDERAL =	33.00%	33.00%	33.00%	33.00%
STATE =	6.60%	6.60%	6.60%	6.60%
TOTAL =	39.60%	39.60%	39.60%	39.60%

property income deduction each year, the Somebodys have managed to retain the 33 percent federal tax bracket despite a 10 percent increase in total income. Their total taxes are estimated to be only $429 more in 1986 than they were in 1983.

Where do they get the money for the leveraged investment? They could use the money they save on taxes each year to pay for the next year's tax shelter. Chapter 19 looks into this area of real estate tax shelters in greater detail.

The Power of Real Estate

In the previous chapter, our hypothetical couple, Mr. and Mrs. Somebody, were considering an investment which would return them 20 percent or more over the next 15 years. How can they find an investment like that? One way is by investing in residential income property.

THE ADVANTAGES OF REAL ESTATE

This can be illustrated very easily. Let us assume that Mr. and Mrs. Somebody borrow the required $25,000 and purchase a $100,000 apartment building. They use the $25,000 as down payment and assume a first mortgage of $75,000 for 30 years at 12 percent. Let's further assume that their monthly rental income will cover the monthly expenses.

We'll also assume a modest 3 percent rate of inflation over the next 15 years, and that after 15 years the Somebodys sell the building for $156,000 ($100,000 compounded at 3 percent for 15 years) and net $81,000 ($156,000 price – $75,000 mortgage = $81,000).

Their return on investment would be over 21 percent ($81,000 profit / $25,000 down payment / 15 years = 21.6 percent).

This return does not take into consideration any increase in rents over the 15 years, nor any deduction of the mortgage principal, not the tax benefits of depreciation.

Carefully acquired and managed income property can keep you way ahead of inflation while providing several other benefits as well. It is not for nothing that real estate is called the IDEAL investment:

I = Interest expense as a tax write-off.
D = Depreciation expense as a tax write-off.
E = Equity build-up over the years.
A = Appreciation of the real estate property.
L = Leverage using other people's money.

In this chapter we will use 1-2-3 to explore various real estate investments. We begin by creating a simple but widely used property-management report which will help you elvaluate income and expenses of potential properties. This type of analysis is frequently done to determine if purchasing a particular piece of property for rental purposes will prove to be a profitable investment. I suggest that you create one of these models for each property you are considering purchasing, and rank them when it comes time to make a choice.

APPRAISING INCOME PROPERTY

Many people have achieved substantial wealth through real estate investments, but they have worked hard at it. The amount of time required to manage real estate can be important to people who are busy or do not want to spend the time watching over their investments. For example, it takes quite a bit of time to manage an apartment building. If you do not want to spend the time, you can invest in a real estate syndicate and let the professionals do the management for you.

If you do want to do it yourself, then it's important to know how to determine value. Before you invest any money in rental real estate, make sure you do a close analysis of the property.

Worksheet 19.2 will help you analyze an investment opportunity. It will show you how to calculate the maximum price to pay, and tell you what the before and after-tax yield will be. It should be used in conjunction with Worksheet 19.1. But first

a few definitions are in order:

Gross Potential Income: total income including rents, garages, laundry, etc., without vacancy factor.

Vacancy Factor: a percentage allowed for vancancies during the year—usually 1 percent to 5 percent of gross rents.

Effecive Gross Income: gross potential income less vacancy and rent loss.

Operating Expenses: total expenses required to operate rentals, including utilities, maintenance, management, etc., usually in the range of 35 percent to 45 percent of income. Does not include mortgage debt service and depreciation.

Net Operating Income (N.O.I.): effective gross income less all operating expenses.

Debit Service: includes interest and principal.

Cash Flow: the net cash remaining after all operating expenses and fixed charges including interest and principal payments, but excluding depreciation and income tax charges.

Depreciation: an allowance or reduction in value resulting from wear and tear, not attributable to land.

Worksheet 19.2 illustrates the acquisition and sale of the property described earlier in this chapter. Most of the real estate formulas are illustrated in the worksheet. The principal payment portion of the mortgage payment can be calculated

---

```
WORKSHEET  19.1:   REAL ESTATE INCOME & EXPENSE


    MARGINS:   LEFT=3, RIGHT=85

    COLUMNS:   GLOBAL=10

    FORMAT:    TEXT

    PRINTER:   COMPRESS=OFF

    RUN    :   AS NEEDED
```

WORKSHEET 19.1: REAL ESTATE INCOME AND EXPENSE FORM
===

```
NAME:          PINEWOOD OAKS APTS     :DATE:     JULY, 1984
LOCATION:         CHARLOTTE, NC       :
TYPE OF PROP:       4 UNITS           :PRICE:    $100,000
-------------------------------------:
ASSESSED VALUE                        :LOANS:    $40,000
  LAND:              $10,000   20%    :
  IMPROVEMENTS:      $40,000   80%    :EQUITY:   $60,000
  TOTAL:             $50,000          :
-------------------------------------:--------------------------
                          FINANCING
EXISTING: BALANCE     PAYMENT  PERIOD  INTEREST   TERM
1ST_____$40,000        $ 380  MONTH    11 %      20 YRS
2ND_____        _____  _____  _____   _____
3RD_____        _____  _____  _____   _____

POTENTIAL:
1ST_____$75,000        $ 771   MO      12 %      30 YRS
```
===

		%	ACTUAL	PROJECTED	COMMENTS
1.	GROSS RENTAL INCOME			16,800	4 X $350 X 12
2.	MISCELLANEOUS INCOME			560	4 GAR $20/mo
3.	TOTAL INCOME	100.00%		17,360	
4.	LESS VACANCY (1%)	1.00%		174	
5.	GROSS OPERATING INCOME	99.00%		17,186	
6.	DEDUCT OPERATING EXPENSES				
7.	ACCOUNTING				
8.	LEGAL				
9.	ADVERTISING	0.86%		150	
10.	LICENSES & PERMITS	0.84%		145	
11.	PROPERTY INSURANCE	2.02%		350	300K Liab.
12.	OWNER'S INSURANCE	1.30%		225	
13.	OTHER INSURANCE				
14.	MANAGEMENT SALARY	9.16%		1,590	Owner Manages
15.	WORKMAN'S COMPENSATION				
16.	SUPPLIES	0.86%		150	
17.	TRAVEL	2.30%		400	
18.	OTHER	0.58%		100	Reserves
19.	REAL ESTATE TAXES	8.64%		1,500	
20.	PERSONAL PROPERTY TAXES	1.15%		200	
21.	REPAIRS	2.59%		450	
22.	MAINTENANCE	4.32%		750	Lawn $60/mo
23.	SERVICES				
24.	ELECTRICITY	1.34%		233	
25.	GAS & OIL	2.46%		427	
26.	SEWER & WATER	3.93%		682	
27.	TELEPHONE	0.20%		35	
28.	MISCELLANEOUS	0.03%		5	
29.	TOTAL OPERATING EXPENSES	42.58%		7,392	
30.	NET OPERATING INCOME	56.42%		9,794	
31.	LESS DEBIT SERVICE	53.29%		9,252	$771 X 12MO
32.	CASH FLOW BEFORE TAXES	3.12%		542	

```
        WORKSHEET 19.2:   REAL ESTATE CASH FLOW ANALYSIS


        MARGINS:   LEFT=3, RIGHT=85

        COLUMNS:   GLOBAL=10

        FORMAT:    TEXT

        PRINTER:   COMPRESS=OFF

        RUN:       AS NEEDED
```

WORKSHEET 19.2:   REAL ESTATE CASH FLOW ANALYSIS

```
================================================================

NAME:        PINEWOOD OAKS APTS        DATE:      JULY, 1984
LOCATION:        CHARLOTTE, NC
TYPE OF PROPERTY:      4 UNITS         PRICE:     $100,000

ASSESSED VALUE:                        LOANS:      $40,000
   LAND:              $10,000
   IMPROVEMENTS:      $40,000          EQUITY      $60,000
   PERSONAL PROP:    ----------
   TOTAL =            $50,000
----------------------------------------------------------------
EXISTING:  BALANCE    PAYMENT    PERIOD    INTEREST    TERM
1ST_____$40,000     $   380    MONTH      11 %     20 YRS
2ND_____   ---------  --------- ---------  ---------
3RD_____   ---------  --------- ---------  ---------

POTENTIAL:
1ST_____$75,000     $   771    MONTH      12 %     30 YRS
================================================================

GROSS POTENTIAL INCOME                     17,360
   LESS VACANCY (Factor = 1%)                 174
                                          ----------
EFFECTIVE GROSS INCOME =                   17,186
   LESS OPERATING EXPENSES                  7,392
                                          ----------
NET OPERATING INCOME =                      9,794
   LESS DEBT SERVICE   ($771 X 12mos)=      9,252
                                          ----------
CASH FLOW BEFORE TAX =                        542
```

```
PLUS PRINCIPAL PAYMENT                              252
LESS DEPRECIATION ($75,000/15 YRS)              (5,000)
                                                ---------
TAXABLE INCOME =                                 (4,206)

  TIMES TAX BRACKET (42%)                        (1,682)
                                                ---------
INCOME TAX PAYABLE =                             (2,523)

  LESS INCOME TAX PAYABLE                              0

AFTER TAX CASH FLOW
  (CASH FLOW - TAX PAYABLE) =                        542
```

as follows: Monthly Mortgage Payment = $771, Mortgage Rate = 12 percent, Mortgage Amount = $75,000:

$771 × 12 mos. = $9,252
$75,000 × 12%   = $9,000
                  - - - -
Principal Amt   = $252

HOW TO DETERMINE
THE VALUE OF A PROPERTY

Worksheet 19.3 is another general real estate model that will assist you in the analysis of real estate.

The *capitalization rate* is one way of calculating value. Most serious professional investors use capitalization rates. The cap rate is a way of determining return on investments. It used to be that investors would not invest their money in real estate unless they could make at least 10 percent return on the investment. In other words, net operating income divided by the price of the property had to be at least 10 percent.

In recent years, however, the values of properties in some parts of the country have been increasing faster than the rate of operating income has been increasing. This has caused the capitalization rates to decline. In California, for example, some investors are willing to purchase real property that has a 5 percent or 4 percent cap rate. This means that they are looking more to an increasing value of property than they are looking for income.

The cap rate can vary from city to city and state to state, but as a general rule it usually lies somewhere between 7 percent and 10 percent. The formulas for the determination of Cap Rate, Income and Value are described on page 155.

```
WORKSHEET  19.3:   REAL ESTATE INVESTMENT ANALYSIS


MARGINS:   LEFT=2, RIGHT=85

COLUMNS:   GLOBAL=10, A=15

FORMAT:    COMMAS NO DECIMALS

PRINTER:   COMPRESS=OFF

RUN:       AS NEEDED
```

WORKSHEET 19.3:   REAL ESTATE INVESTMENT ANALYSIS

ASSUMPTIONS:

PURCHASE PRICE		$630,000
FIRST MORTGAGE	70.00%	$441,000
DOWN PAYMENT		$189,000
INTEREST RATE & AMT	8.50%	$37,485
ANNUAL PAYMENT (P&I)		$41,035
ALLOCATION TO LAND	20.00%	$126,000
AMOUNT DEPRECIATED		$504,000
NO. YEAR SL DEPRECIATION		15

GROSS POTENTIAL INCOME		$100,000
LESS VACANCY	12.50%	$12,500

EFFECTIVE GROSS INCOME =		$87,500
LESS OPERATING EXPENSES		$31,000

NET OPERATING INCOME =		$56,500
LESS DEBT SERVICE		$41,035

CASH FLOW BEFORE TAX =		$15,465
PLUS PRINCIPAL PAYMENT		$3,550
LESS DEPRECIATION		($33,600)

TAXABLE INCOME =		($14,585)
TIMES TAX BRACKET	42.00%	

INCOME TAX PAYABLE =	($6,126)
AFTER TAX CASH FLOW	
(CASH FLOW – TAX PAYABLE) =	$21,590
CAP RATE =	8.97%
VALUE =	$630,000
INCOME =	$56,500
CASH ON CASH RETURN =	8.18%
EQUITY RATE OF RETURN =	10.06%

Cap Rate = Income (N.O.I.) / Value (Market or Cost).

Value = Income (N.O.I.) / Cap Rate.

Income (N.O.I.) = Value × Cap Rate.

Cash on Cash Return = Cash Flow / Down payment.

PERCENT Return on Equity = Cash Flow / Equity.

WHICH HOME
MORTGAGE OFFERS THE BEST VALUE?

The great American dream has long been to own one's own home. But in recent years, the complications of financing a home purchase have prevented vast numbers of people from realizing that dream. With more financing programs available than ever before, today's homebuyer is faced with a complex set of options before purchasing a new home. It often is difficult, if not impossible, to decide which package is the best financially and practically.

Worksheet 19.4 will help you analyze different methods of home financing and quickly provide you with a close approximation of the tax advantages whenever you consider buying a home. Owning a home can offer very attractive financial benefits. The interest you pay on the mortgage, as well as the property taxes, will provide substantial deductions on your income tax return. This can result in a substantially lower federal income tax, and the money saved on taxes can be applied toward your housing costs.

Worksheet 19.4 is preprogrammed so that a home buyer can see what the monthly payments will be on a particular piece of property and how much cash will be needed for the down payment and the close of escrow.

The worksheet also will estimate the tax savings based on your income tax bracket. This is displayed as the effective monthly payment, i.e., the actual out-of-pocket amount after claiming the tax deductions allowed for purchase a home. For example, if a family with a combined income of $55,000 purchases a $100,000, 80 percent, 30-year fixed rate (14 percent) loan on a $125,000 house, they would have a monthly payment of $1,190 (principal and interest). Based on their 40 percent tax bracket, though, the effective after-tax net payment would be only $714—a difference of $476 a month.

The worksheet allows you to change the terms of the loan, adjust the down payment, and calculate or directly enter the closing costs. The formulas for calculating the amount of monthly payment and the effective after-tax net payment are as follows:

(@PMT(100000,.14,30))/12

$1,190*(1 − .40)

A CHECKLIST FOR CLOSING COSTS

If you've ever bought a house, you have gone through a ceremony called the closing, settlement, or close of escrow, depending on the part of the country in which you live. A hodgepodge of local customs dictates how closing costs are handled, but it is not uncommon for the lender to expect you to reimburse him for the legal expenses involved in preparing the papers, for the credit bureau costs involved in checking your credit history, for out-of-pocket expenses for appraisals on the property, and for the cost of the title search that the lender conducts for his own benefit. Each locality has its own rules regarding closing costs, so it's best to check with your local real estate agent or lender to find out the procedures for your area.

Closing costs can amount to a few thousand dollars and usually are paid at the time of settlement. It's difficult to say what closing costs will run, but a ballpark estimate might be 2 or 3 percent of the loan amount. That doesn't include the discount points charged on the loan, the real estate commissions, or the remainder of the down payment above the earnest money deposit.

In response to consumer complaints regarding real estate closing costs and procedures, Congress passed the Real Estate Settlement Procedures Act

WORKSHEET 19.4: HOME PURCHASE ANALYZER

MARGINS: LEFT=5, RIGHT=75

COLUMNS: GLOBAL=10, A=25

PRINTER: COMPRESS=OFF

RUN: AS NEEDED

HOMES   22-Oct-84

WORKSHEET 19.4: HOME PURCHASE ANALYZER

SALES PRICE $125,000
LOAN TO VALUE RATIO   80.00%
MORTGAGE AMOUNT $100,000

SECOND MORTGAGE
DOWNPAYMENT $25,000

LENDER INTEREST RATE   14.00%
POINTS   3.00% $3,000
AMORTIZATION - YEARS   30

MONTHLY PAYMENT = $1,190
  (@PMT(100000,.14,30))/12

PLUS: PROPERTY TAX   1.00% $1,250   104

MORTGAGE & PROP TAX (BEFORE TAX) = $1,294
                                               ======

TAX BRACKET   42.00%
EFFECTIVE NET PAYMENT (AFTER TAX) = $751
                                                =====

   PLUS HOMEOWNER'S INSURANCE $360 $30

TOTAL MONTHLY PAYMENT (AFTER TAX) = $781
                                               ====

ESTIMATED CASH REQUIRED:

DOWN PAYMENT $25,000
POINTS $3,000
OTHER CLOSING COSTS $2,285

     TOTAL DOWN PAYMENT REQUIRED = $30,285
                                              ========

156

(RESPA) of 1974. This act prohibits kickbacks and fees for services not performed during the close of escrow. For example, it's illegal for attorneys and escrow agents to channel title business to a certain title company in return for a fee.

Perhaps the most obvious benefits of RESPA to the typical home buyer are that:

1. The buyer will receive from the lender a Department of Housing and Urban Development booklet explaining RESPA.

2. The buyer will receive a good-faith estimate of closing costs from the lender.

3. The lender will use the HUD Uniform Settlement Statement Form.

```
WORKSHEET  19.5:   GOOD-FAITH ESTIMATE OF CLOSING COSTS


    MARGINS:   LEFT=5, RIGHT=75

    COLUMNS:   A=30, B=10

    PRINTER:   COMPRESS=OFF

    RUN:       AS NEEDED
```

```
CLOSING                                22-Oct-84

WORKSHEET 19.5:  GOOD-FAITH ESTIMATE OF CLOSING COSTS
--------------------------------------------------------
SERVICES                              !  EST. FEES
========================================================
                                      !
LOAN ORIGINATION FEE                  !    3,000.00
APPRAISAL FEE                         !      100.00
CREDIT REPORT                         !       25.00
MORTGAGE ASSUMPTION FEE               !
MORTGAGE INSURANCE PREMIUM            !
PRORATIONS: TAXES                     !    1,250.00
            INSURANCE                 !      100.00
            INTEREST                  !
TITLE INSURANCE                       !      300.00
ESCROW FEES                           !
TERMITE INSPECTION                    !       45.00
BUILDING INSPECTION                   !
FIRE INSURANCE                        !      200.00
RECORDING FEES                        !       15.00
NOTARY FEES                           !
ATTORNEY'S FEES                       !      250.00
                                      !-------------
                                      !   $5,285.00
```

4. The borrower has the right to inspect the statement one business day before the day of closing.

The primary reason lenders are required to give loan applicants a prompt estimate of closing costs is to allow the loan applicant an opportunity to compare prices. Additionally, these estimates help the borrower calculate how much his closing costs will be.

Worksheet 19.5 illustrates a good-faith estimate form. This example covers many, but not all, items that may be required at settlement.

SECTION 7

GETTING GOOD RESULTS

How Do You
Know You're On Target?

If you have a color monitor on your home computer and you are using Lotus 1-2-3 or Symphony to construct the worksheets in this book, you will want to use their powerful graphics commands. If you don't have a graphics monitor, however, the Lotus programs do have a GRAPH program that allows you to print or plot graphs saved as files using the /GRAPH SAVE command. The graphics modules come on a separate disk, and the commands follow the same format as the Lotus program.

HOW TO EVALUATE YOUR NET WORTH

An example of this graphing function is illustrated below on a graph which plots Mr. Somebody's net worth from Worksheet 20.1. The graph shows the actual growth of net worth for the past five years and projects the growth for the next five years. It also plots the growth in the Consumer Price Index for the years 1980 through 1988.

Worksheet 20.1 was created by retrieving the net worth information from Worksheet 12.5 and then editing out the unnecessary data. Remember to take out any extraneous spaces and vertical lines before graphing the data; otherwise you will get spaces and distortions in your printout.

In order to graph Worksheet 20.1 you first select the type of graph, in this case a line graph. Then specify the *"A"* range of data values as the Total Net Worth Line.

The annual percent increase of the Consumer Price Index is entered for each year and multiplied by the preceding annual net worth figure. For example, with 1979 as our base year, we multiply the 12 percent increase in the 1980 CPI by the 1979 total net worth of $40,000 to get the $44,800 as the starting CPI graph value for the B range.

You can add labels to your graph by selecting the years 1979 to 1988 as the **X** Range of entries in the worksheet. Titles can be added at the top of the graph.

Save and name the graph with the /GRAPH SAVE command. Then replace your Lotus 1-2-3 disk with the Print Graph disk. The instructions for using this program are in the appendix of the Lotus 1-2-3 manual.

WORKSHEET 20.1: GRAPHING NET WORTH

MARGINS: LEFT=2, RIGHT=132

COLUMNS: GLOBAL=10

FORMAT: COMMAS, NO DECIMALS

PRINTER: COMPRESS=ON

RUN AT: YEAR END

WORKSHEET 20.1: GRAPHING CPI VS NET WORTH

ASSET	1979	1980	1981	1982	1983	1984	1985	1986	1987	1988
NET WORTH	$40,000	$42,200	$47,100	$52,700	$58,000	$61,640	$65,538	$69,716	$74,196	$79,003
CPI PERCENT	0.00%	12.00%	10.00%	4.00%	4.00%	4.00%	4.00%	4.00%	4.00%	4.00%
GRAPH VALUE	$40,000	$44,800	$49,280	$51,251	$53,301	$55,433	$57,651	$59,957	$62,355	$64,849

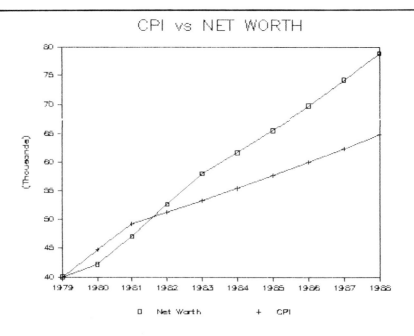

CPI vs NET WORTH

□ Net Worth   + CPI

162

Appendix

Selected Lotus 1-2-3
Worksheet Cell Formulas

Included in this appendix are cell formulas for the following worksheets:

```
A1: 'WORKSHEET  9.1:   PERSONAL        A8:  \=
FINANCIAL STATEMENT                    B8:  \=
A2: \-                                 C8:  \=
B2: \-                                 D8:  \=
C2: \-                                 E8:  \=
D2: \-                                 F8:  \=
E2: \-                                 G8:  \=
F2: \-                                 A9:  ^ASSETS
G2: \-                                 B9:  ^¦
B3: 'PERSONAL FINANCIAL STATEMENT      C9:  ^AMOUNT
... AS OF ...                          D9:  ^¦¦
F3: (D1) @TODAY                        E9:  ^LIABILITIES
B5: 'JAMES T. SOMEBODY                 F9:  ^¦
E5: "500 ALL-AMERICAN WAY              G9:  ^AMOUNT
B6: 'JUDY R. SOMEBODY                  A10: \-
E6: 'ANYTOWN, USA  94123               B10: \-
E7: "(465) 987-4321                    C10: \-
```

164

```
D10: \-                          A25: "   Other properties
E10: \-                          C25: (,0) +G214
F10: \-                          D25: ^¦¦
G10: \-                          E25: "   Vacation property
A11: 'CASH                       G25: (,0) +F214
D11: ^¦¦                         A26: "   IRA or KEOGH
E11: 'CURRENT BILLS              C26: (,0) +G140
A12: "   Checking accounts       D26: ^¦¦
C12: (,0) +G113+G114+G115        E26: "   Other properties
D12: ^¦¦                         A27: "   Equity in business
E12: "   Mortgage or rent        D27: ^¦¦
G12: (,0) 550                    D28: ^¦¦
A13: "   Savings accounts        A29: 'PERSONAL PROPERTY
C13: (,0) +G116                  D29: ^¦¦
D13: ^¦¦                         E29: 'TAXES DUE
E13: "   Charge accts            A30: "   Automobiles
G13: (,0) 150                    C30: (,0) 12000
A14: "   Money-market funds      D30: ^¦¦
C14: (,0) +G117                  E30: '   Federal
D14: ^¦¦                         G30: (,0) 3000
E14: "   Credit cards            A31: "   Household furniture
G14: (,0) 1250                   C31: (,0) 15000
A15: "   Life insurance cash val D31: ^¦¦
D15: ^¦¦                         E31: '   State
E15: '   Other bills             G31: (,0) 0
D16: ^¦¦                         A32: "   Collectibles
A17: 'MARKETABLE SECURITIES      C32: (,0) 1000
D17: ^¦¦                         D32: ^¦¦
E17: 'LOANS                      E32: '   Local
A18: '   Stocks                  A33: '   Other
C18: (,0) +G127+G128             C33: (,0) 5500
D18: ^¦¦                         D33: ^¦¦
E18: '   Auto                    E33: '   Other
G18: (,0) +G234                  D34: ^¦¦
A19: '   Bonds                   A35: 'TOTAL ASSETS
D19: ^¦¦                         C35: (,0) @SUM(C33..C11)
E19: "   Education               D35: ^¦¦
A20: "   Gov't securities        E35: 'TOTAL LIABILITIES
C20: (,0) +G126                  G35: (,0) @SUM(G33..G12)
D20: ^¦¦                         D36: ^¦¦
E20: "   Sailboat                D37: ^¦¦
G20: (,0) +G233                  E37: 'NET WORTH
A21: "   Mutual funds            G37: (,0) +C35-G35
D21: ^¦¦                         A38: \=
E21: '   Other                   B38: \=
D22: ^¦¦                         C38: \=
A23: 'NON-LIQUID INVESTMENTS     D38: \=
D23: ^¦¦                         E38: \=
E23: 'MORTAGES                   F38: \=
A24: "   Real estate: home       G38: \=
C24: (,0) +G213                  A39: "      ANNUAL SOURCES OF INCOME
D24: ^¦¦                         D39: ^¦¦
E24: '   Home                    E39: "    PERSONAL INFORMATION
G24: (,0) +F213                  A40: \-
```

```
B40:  \-                          D52:  ^¦¦
C40:  \-                          E52:  'DEFENDENT IN ANY SUITS?      No
D40:  \-                          D53:  ^¦¦
E40:  \-                          E53:  'EVER TAKEN BANKRUPTCY?      No
F40:  \-                          A54:  \=
G40:  \-                          B54:  \=
A41:  'SALARY: James              C54:  \=
C41:  (,0) 31000                  D54:  \=
D41:  ^¦¦                         E54:  \=
E41:  'OCCUPATION                 F54:  \=
G41:  ^AGE                        G54:  \=
A42:  'BUS. INCOME: Judy          A55:  'THE UNDERSIGNED CERTIFIES
C42:  (,0) 15000                  THAT THE INFORMATION HEREIN IS
D42:  ^¦¦                         TRUE
A43:  'OTHER INCOME               A56:  'AND ACCURATE AS OF THIS DATE.
C43:  (,0) 1000                   A58:  'DATE _____
D43:  ^¦¦                         D58:  "           SIGNATURE _____
E43:  'James: Executive           _____
G43:  ^40                         D59:  "           SIGNATURE _____
A44:  'INTEREST                   _____
C44:  (,0) 300                    A100: 'WORKSHEET  9.2A:   SUPPLE
D44:  ^¦¦                         MENTARY SCHEDULES
A45:  'DIVIDENDS                  A101: \-
C45:  (,0) 400                    B101: \-
D45:  ^¦¦                         C101: \-
E45:  'Judy: Decorator            D101: \-
G45:  ^38                         E101: \-
D46:  ^¦¦                         F101: \-
A47:  'TOTAL INCOME               G101: \-
C47:  (,0) @SUM(C41..C45)         B102: 'SUPPLEMENTARY SCHEDULES NO.
D47:  ^¦¦                         1 ... AS OF ...
E47:  'MINOR CHILDREN: 2          F102: (D1) @TODAY
G47:  "6 AND 10                   B104: 'JAMES T. SOMEBODY
A48:  \=                          E104: "500 ALL-AMERICAN WAY
B48:  \=                          B105: 'JUDY R. SOMEBODY
C48:  \=                          E105: 'ANYTOWN, USA 94123
D48:  \=                          E106: "(465) 987-4321
E48:  \=                          A108: \=
F48:  \=                          B108: \=
G48:  \=                          C108: \=
A49:  "       CONTINGENT LIABILITIES  D108: \=
D49:  ^¦¦                         E108: \=
E49:  "       GENERAL INFORMATION F108: \=
A50:  \-                          G108: \=
B50:  \-                          B109: 'SCHEDULE A:  CASH AND BANK
C50:  \-                          ACCOUNTS
D50:  \-                          A110: \-
E50:  \-                          B110: \-
F50:  \-                          C110: \-
G50:  \-                          D110: \-
A51:  'AS ENDORSER OR CO-MAKER?   E110: \-
No                               F110: \-
D51:  ^¦¦                         G110: \-
E51:  'ANY ASSETS PLEDGED?      No
```

```
A111: 'BANK NAME
C111: 'LOCATION
E111: 'HELD BY
F111: ^ACCT NO.
G111: "AMOUNT
A112: \-
B112: \-
C112: \-
D112: \-
E112: \-
F112: \-
G112: \-
A113: 'National Bank
C113: 'Anytown, USA
E113: 'James
F113: "198748-67
G113: (,0) 250
A114: 'Stagecoach Bank
C114: 'Anytown, USA
E114: 'Joint
F114: "67398-21
G114: (,0) 500
A115: 'Country Bank
C115: 'Anytown, USA
E115: 'Judy
F115: "20987-667
G115: (,0) 250
A116: "First S&L Assoc
C116: 'Anytown, USA
E116: 'Joint
F116: "1-15257-03
G116: (,0) 5000
A117: 'CrUn MoneyMktFnd
C117: 'Anytown, USA
E117: 'Joint
F117: "557632
G117: 2000
G118: "------
E119: 'TOTAL CASH ON HAND =
G119: (CO) @SUM(G117..G113)
A121: \=
B121: \=
C121: \=
D121: \=
E121: \=
F121: \=
G121: \=
B122: 'SCHEDULE B:  STOCKS, BONDS
AND OTHER SECURITIES
A123: \-
B123: \-
C123: \-
D123: \-
E123: \-

F123: \-
G123: \-
A124: 'DESCRIPTION
C124: ^DATE
D124: ^HELD BY
E124: ^#SHRS
F124: "COST
G124: "MKT VALUE
A125: \-
B125: \-
C125: \-
D125: \-
E125: \-
F125: \-
G125: \-
A126: 'US Gov't Securties
C126: (D1) @DATE(82,2,18)
D126: ^Joint
E126: ^100
F126: (,0) 5000
G126: (,0) 3000
A127: 'Nxxon
C127: (D1) @DATE(83,5,24)
D127: ^Joint
E127: ^100
F127: (,0) 3500
G127: (,0) 4000
A128: 'Global Oil
C128: (D1) @DATE(84,8,27)
D128: ^Joint
E128: ^100
F128: (,0) 1000
G128: (,0) 2500
G129: "------
E130: 'TOTAL MARKET VALUE =
G130: (CO) @SUM(G128..G126)
A132: \=
B132: \=
C132: \=
D132: \=
E132: \=
F132: \=
G132: \=
B133: 'SCHEDULE C:  IRA AND KEOGH
ACCOUNTS
A134: \-
B134: \-
C134: \-
D134: \-
E134: \-
F134: \-
G134: \-
A135: 'DESCRIPTION
C135: ^DATE
```

```
D135:  ^HELD BY                      D210:  \-
E135:  ^UNITS                        E210:  \-
F135:  "COST                         F210:  \-
G135:  "MKT VALUE                    G210:  \-
A136:  \-                            A211:  'DESCRIPTION
B136:  \-                            C211:  ^DATE
C136:  \-                            D211:  ^HELD BY
D136:  \-                            E211:  "COST
E136:  \-                            F211:  "MORTGAGE
F136:  \-                            G211:  "MKT VALUE
G136:  \-                            A212:  \-
A137:  'Drey's Group                 B212:  \-
C137:  (D1) @DATE(83,6,2)            C212:  \-
D137:  ^Joint                        D212:  \-
E137:  ^200                          E212:  \-
F137:  (,0) 2000                     F212:  \-
G137:  (,0) 3000                     G212:  \-
A138:  'Bank CD's                    A213:  'Residence
C138:  (D1) @DATE(84,1,4)            C213:  (D1) @DATE(76,5,8)
D138:  ^Joint                        D213:  ^Joint
E138:  ^10                           E213:  (,0) 50000
F138:  (,0) 2000                     F213:  (,0) 30000
G138:  (,0) 2500                     G213:  (,0) 110000
G139:  "------                       A214:  'Vacation cabin
E140:  'TOTAL MARKET VALUE =         C214:  (D1) @DATE(79,2,3)
G140:  (C0) @SUM(G139..G137)         D214:  ^Joint
                                     E214:  (,0) 25000
A200:  'WORKSHEET 9.2B:   SUPPLE     F214:  (,0) 21000
MENTARY SCHEDULES                    G214:  (,0) 35000
A201:  \-                            E215:  "------
B201:  \-                            F215:  "------
C201:  \-                            G215:  "------
D201:  \-                            D216:  "TOTAL =
E201:  \-                            E216:  (C0) @SUM(E213..E214)
F201:  \-                            F216:  (C0) @SUM(F213..F214)
G201:  \-                            G216:  (C0) @SUM(G213..G214)
B202:  'SUPPLEMENTARY SCHEDULES NO.  A218:  \=
2 ... AS OF ...                      B218:  \=
F202:  (D1) @TODAY                   C218:  \=
B204:  'JAMES T. SOMEBODY            D218:  \=
E204:  "500 ALL-AMERICAN WAY         E218:  \=
B205:  'JUDY R. SOMEBODY             F218:  \=
E205:  'ANYTOWN, USA 94123           G218:  \=
E206:  "(456) 987-4321               B219:  'SCHEDULE E:   LIFE INSURANCE
A208:  \=                            A220:  \-
B208:  \=                            B220:  \-
C208:  \=                            C220:  \-
D208:  \=                            D220:  \-
E208:  \=                            E220:  \-
F208:  \=                            F220:  \-
G208:  \=                            G220:  \-
B209:  'SCHEDULE D:   REAL ESTATE    A221:  'INSURED
A210:  \-                            C221:  'POLICY
B210:  \-                            D221:  'BENEFICARY
C210:  \-
```

```
E221: 'INSURANCE CO                      A234: 'Country Bank
G221: 'FACE AMOUNT                       C234: (D1) @DATE(82,6,9)
A222: \-                                 D234: '       Honda '82
B222: \-                                 F234: (,0) 9000
C222: \-                                 G234: (,0) 5000
D222: \-                                 G235: "------
E222: \-                                 F236: 'TOTAL =
F222: \-                                 G236: (CO) @SUM(G234..G233)
G222: \-                                 A1: 'TAXPROJ
A223: 'James Somebody                    C1: (D1) @TODAY
C223: 'Term
D223: 'Wife                              A3: 'WORKSHEET   13.3   PROJECTION
E223: 'Trudential                        OF INCOME TAXES
G223: (,0) 150000                        A5: \-
A224: 'Judy Somebody                     B5: \-
C224: 'Term                              C5: \-
D224: 'Husband                           A6: 'GROSS INCOME
E224: 'Conn Corp.                        B6: "1983
G224: (,0) 50000                         C6: "1984
G225: "------                            A7: \-
G226: (CO) @SUM(G225..G223)              B7: \-
A228: \=                                 C7: \-
B228: \=                                 A9: 'Salary
C228: \=                                 B9: (,0) 31000
D228: \=                                 C9: (,0) 1.1*B9
E228: \=                                 A10: 'Interest
F228: \=                                 B10: (,0) 300
G228: \=                                 C10: (,0) 325
B229: 'SCHEDULE F:  FINANCIAL            A11: 'Dividend
CREDIT INFORMATION                       B11: (,0) 400
A230: \-                                 C11: (,0) 425
B230: \-                                 A12: 'State tax refund
C230: \-                                 B12: (,0) 412
D230: \-                                 C12: (,0) 450
E230: \-                                 A13: 'Business income
F230: \-                                 B13: (,0) 15000
G230: \-                                 C13: (,0) 17500
A231: 'NAME OF INSTITUTION               A14: 'Property income
C231: ^DATE                              B14: (,0) -1592
D231: '      PURPOSE                     C14: (,0) -2000
F231: 'ORIG AMOUNT                       A15: 'Capital gains
G231: "BALANCE                           B15: (,0) 2180
A232: \-                                 C15: (,0) 2200
B232: \-                                 A16: \-
C232: \-                                 B16: (,0) \-
D232: \-                                 C16: (,0) \-
E232: \-                                 A17: '1. TOTAL INCOME
F232: \-                                 B17: (,0) @SUM(B16..B9)
G232: \-                                 C17: (,0) @SUM(C16..C9)
A233: 'Credit Union                      A19: 'DEDUCTIONS
C233: (D1) @DATE(84,3,21)                A20: '----------------
D233: '     Sailboat                     A21: 'Move expenses
F233: (,0) 5500                          B21: (,0) 0
G233: (,0) 5000                          C21: (,0) 0
                                         A22: 'Business expense
```

B22: (,0) 2063
C22: (,0) 2200
A23: 'IRA/KEOGH
B23: (,0) 2000
C23: (,0) 4000
A24: \-
B24: (,0) \-
C24: (,0) \-
A25: '2. ADJUSTED GROSS
B25: (,0) +B17-@SUM(B21..B23)
C25: (,0) +C17-@SUM(C21..C23)
A28: 'Medical expenses
B28: (,0) 147
C28: (,0) 200
A29: 'State sales tax
B29: (,0) 1099
C29: (,0) 1200
A30: 'Interest expense
B30: (,0) 5108
C30: (,0) 5200
A31: 'Charity
B31: (,0) 385
C31: (,0) 425
A32: 'Misc deductions
B32: (,0) 701
C32: (,0) 775
A33: 'Zero tax bracket
B33: (,0) -3400
C33: (,0) -3400
A34: 'Exemptions x 1000
B34: (,0) 4000
C34: (,0) 4000
A35: \-
B35: (,0) \-
C35: (,0) \-
A36: '3. TAXABLE INCOME
B36: (,0) +B25-@SUM(B28..B34)
C36: (,0) +C25-@SUM(C28..C34)
A38: 'Total tax
B38: (,0) 6763
C38: (,0) 7330
A39: 'Tax credit
B39: (,0) 0
C39: (,0) 0
A40: \-
B40: (,0) \-
C40: (,0) \-
A41: '4. TAXES:FEDERAL=
B41: (CO) +B38-B39
C41: (CO) +C38-C39
A42: "STATE =
B42: (CO) 0.2*B41
C42: (CO) 0.2*C41
B43: (CO) "------

C43: (CO) "------
A44: "TOTAL TAXES =
B44: (CO) +B42+B41
C44: (CO) +C42+C41
A46: "TAXES/INCOME =
B46: (P2) +B44/B17
C46: (P2) +C44/C17
A49: "TAX BRACKET:
A50: "FEDERAL =
B50: (P2) 0.35
C50: (P2) 0.33
A51: "STATE =
B51: (P2) 0.2*+B50
C51: (P2) 0.2*+C50
B52: (P2) "------
C52: (P2) "------
A53: "TOTAL =
B53: (P2) +B51+B50
C53: (P2) +C51+C50
A1: 'RETPROJ
D1: (D1) @TODAY
___

A3: 'WORKSHEET 16.3: PROJECTION
OF NET WORTH AT RETIREMENT
A4: \-
B4: \-
C4: \-
D4: \-
A5: 'ASSUMPTIONS:
A6: " FINANCIAL GOAL =
C6: (CO) 1000000
A7: " YEARS TIL RETIREMENT =
C7: 25
A9: 'ANNUAL CONTRIBUTIONS:
A10: '   SAVINGS =
C10: (CO) 1000
A11: '   IRA/KEOGH =
C11: (CO) 3000
A12: '   MONEY MARKET =
C12: (CO) 1000
A13: '   COMPANY STOCK =
C13: (CO) 2000
A14: \-
B14: \-
C14: \-
D14: \-
A15: 'ASSETS
B15: "PRESENT
C15: "% GROWTH
D15: "RETIREMENT $
A16: \-
B16: \-
C16: \-
D16: \-
A17: 'SAVINGS

```
B17: (,0) 6000                        B35: (,0) 21000
C17: (P2) 0.08                        D35: (,0) 0
D17: (,0) @FV($C$10,$C$17,$C$7)       A36: 'TAXES
A18: 'IRA/KEOGH                       B36: (,0) 3000
B18: (,0) 5500                        D36: 0
C18: (P2) 0.12                        A37: \-
D18: (,0) @FV($C$11,$C$18,$C$7)       B37: (,0) \-
A19: 'MONEY MARKET                    C37: \-
B19: (,0) 2000                        D37: (,0) \-
C19: (P2) 0.08                        A38: 'TOTALS=
D19: (,0) @FV($C$12,$C$19,$C$7)       B38: (C0) @SUM(B37..B31)
A20: 'COMPANY STOCK                   D38: (C0) @SUM(D35..D31)
B20: (,0) 6500                        A42: 'NET WORTH =
C20: (P2) 0.09                        B42: (C0) +B25-B38
D20: (,0) @FV($C$13,$C$20,$C$7)       D42: (C0) +D25-D38
A21: 'BONDS                           B43: "========
B21: (,0) 3000                        D43: (,0) "==========
C21: (P2) 0.05                        A1: 'STKYIELD
D21: (,0) (+B21)*(1+C21)^$C$7         G1: (D1) @TODAY
A22: 'REAL ESTATE                     _____
B22: (,0) 145000                      A3: 'WORKSHEET   17.3A:   ANALYSIS
C22: (P2) 0.03                        OF MONTHLY STOCK PURCHASE
D22: (,0) (+B22)*(1+C22)^$C$7         A4: \-
A23: 'PERSONAL                        B4: \-
B23: (,0) 33500                       C4: \-
C23: (P2) 0.01                        D4: \-
D23: (,0) (+B23)*(1+C23)^$C$7         E4: \-
A24: \-                               F4: \-
B24: (,0) \-                          G4: \-
C24: \-                               H4: \-
D24: (,0) \-                          C6: '       JAMES  T.  SOMEBODY
A25: 'TOTALS=                         C8: '   MONTHLY STOCK PURCHASE PLAN
B25: (C0) @SUM(B23..B17)              C9: 'SALES MARKETING CORPORATION
D25: (C0) @SUM(D24..D16)              (SMC)
A29: 'LIABILITIES                     B11: "   PRICE AS OF
B29: (,0) "PRESENT                    D11: (D1) @TODAY
D29: (,0) "RETIREMENT $               E11: (C2) ' EQUALS
A30: \-                               F11: (C2) 78
B30: (,0) \-                          C12: 'QUARTERLY DIVIDEND
C30: \-                               E12: ' EQUALS
D30: (,0) \-                          F12: (C2) 0.7
A31: 'CURR BILLS                      A15: ^DATE OF
B31: (,0) 1950                        C15: ^UNIT
D31: (,0) 0                           D15: ^TOTAL
A32: 'AUTO LOANS                      E15: ^TODAY'S
B32: (,0) 5000                        F15: ^YIELD
D32: (,0) 0                           G15: ^TOTAL
A33: 'OTHER LOANS                     H15: ^PERCENT
B33: (,0) 5000                        A16: ^PURCHASE
D33: (,0) 0                           B16: ^#SHRS
A34: 'HOME MTG                        C16: ^COST
B34: (,0) 30000                       D16: ^COST
D34: (,0) 0                           E16: ^VALUE
A35: 'CABIN MTG                       F16: ^ON COST
                                      G16: ^RETURN
```

```
H16:  ^RETURN                              F23:  (P2)  (+$F$12*4)/C23
A17:  \-                                   G23:  (,2)  +B23*(AA23+$F$11)-D23
B17:  \-                                   H23:  (P2)  +G23/D23
C17:  \-                                   A24:  (D1)  @DATE(83,3,31)
D17:  \-                                   B24:  2
E17:  \-                                   C24:  (,2)  75.38
F17:  \-                                   D24:  (,2)  +B24*C24
G17:  \-                                   E24:  (,2)  +$F$11*B24
H17:  \-                                   F24:  (P2)  (+$F$12*4)/C24
A18:  (D1)  @DATE(83,1,15)                 G24:  (,2)  +B24*(AA24+$F$11)-D24
B18:  3                                    H24:  (P2)  +G24/D24
C18:  (,2)  60.31                          A25:  (D1)  @DATE(83,3,31)
D18:  (,2)  +B18*C18                       B25:  2
E18:  (,2)  +$F$11*B18                     C25:  (,2)  87.77
F18:  (P2)  (+$F$12*4)/C18                 D25:  (,2)  +B25*C25
G18:  (,2)  +B18*(AA18+$F$11)-D18          E25:  (,2)  +$F$11*B25
H18:  (P2)  +G18/D18                       F25:  (P2)  (+$F$12*4)/C25
A19:  (D1)  @DATE(83,1,21)                 G25:  (,2)  +B25*(AA25+$F$11)-D25
B19:  1                                    H25:  (P2)  +G25/D25
C19:  (,2)  61.3                           A26:  (D1)  @DATE(83,4,15)
D19:  (,2)  +B19*C19                       B26:  2
E19:  (,2)  +$F$11*B19                     C26:  (,2)  73.56
F19:  (P2)  (+$F$12*4)/C19                 D26:  (,2)  +B26*C26
G19:  (,2)  +B19*(AA19+$F$11)-D19          E26:  (,2)  +$F$11*B26
H19:  (P2)  +G19/D19                       F26:  (P2)  (+$F$12*4)/C26
A20:  (D1)  @DATE(83,1,31)                 G26:  (,2)  +B26*(AA26+$F$11)-D26
B20:  2                                    H26:  (P2)  +G26/D26
C20:  (,2)  63.15                          A27:  (D1)  @DATE(83,4,29)
D20:  (,2)  +B20*C20                       B27:  1
E20:  (,2)  +$F$11*B20                     C27:  (,2)  79.3
F20:  (P2)  (+$F$12*4)/C20                 D27:  (,2)  +B27*C27
G20:  (,2)  +B20*(AA20+$F$11)-D20          E27:  (,2)  +$F$11*B27
H20:  (P2)  +G20/D20                       F27:  (P2)  (+$F$12*4)/C27
A21:  (D1)  @DATE(83,2,15)                 G27:  (,2)  +B27*(AA27+$F$11)-D27
B21:  2                                    H27:  (P2)  +G27/D27
C21:  (,2)  64.69                          A28:  (D1)  @DATE(83,5,13)
D21:  (,2)  +B21*C21                       B28:  2
E21:  (,2)  +$F$11*B21                     C28:  (,2)  78.71
F21:  (P2)  (+$F$12*4)/C21                 D28:  (,2)  +B28*C28
G21:  (,2)  +B21*(AA21+$F$11)-D21          E28:  (,2)  +$F$11*B28
H21:  (P2)  +G21/D21                       F28:  (P2)  (+$F$12*4)/C28
A22:  (D1)  @DATE(83,2,28)                 G28:  (,2)  +B28*(AA28+$F$11)-D28
B22:  2                                    H28:  (P2)  +G28/D28
C22:  (,2)  84.79                          A29:  (D1)  @DATE(83,5,15)
D22:  (,2)  +B22*C22                       B29:  1
E22:  (,2)  +$F$11*B22                     C29:  (,2)  74.13
F22:  (P2)  (+$F$12*4)/C22                 D29:  (,2)  +B29*C29
G22:  (,2)  +B22*(AA22+$F$11)-D22          E29:  (,2)  +$F$11*B29
H22:  (P2)  +G22/D22                       F29:  (P2)  (+$F$12*4)/C29
A23:  (D1)  @DATE(83,3,15)                 G29:  (,2)  +B29*(AA29+$F$11)-D29
B23:  2                                    H29:  (P2)  +G29/D29
C23:  (,2)  85.38                          A30:  (D1)  @DATE(83,5,31)
D23:  (,2)  +B23*C23                       B30:  2
E23:  (,2)  +$F$11*B23                     C30:  (,2)  64.83
```

```
D30:  (,2)  +B30*C30
E30:  (,2)  +$F$11*B30
F30:  (P2)  (+$F$12*4)/C30
G30:  (,2)  +B30*(AA30+$F$11)-D30
H30:  (P2)  +G30/D30
A31:  (D1)  @DATE(83,6,15)
B31:  2
C31:  (,2)  64.63
D31:  (,2)  +B31*C31
E31:  (,2)  +$F$11*B31
F31:  (P2)  (+$F$12*4)/C31
G31:  (,2)  +B31*(AA31+$F$11)-D31
H31:  (P2)  +G31/D31
A32:  (D1)  @DATE(83,6,30)
B32:  1
C32:  (,2)  62.32
D32:  (,2)  +B32*C32
E32:  (,2)  +$F$11*B32
F32:  (P2)  (+$F$12*4)/C32
G32:  (,2)  +B32*(AA32+$F$11)-D32
H32:  (P2)  +G32/D32
A33:  (D1)  @DATE(83,7,15)
B33:  2
C33:  (,2)  63.54
D33:  (,2)  +B33*C33
E33:  (,2)  +$F$11*B33
F33:  (P2)  (+$F$12*4)/C33
G33:  (,2)  +B33*(AA33+$F$11)-D33
H33:  (P2)  +G33/D33
A34:  (D1)  @DATE(83,7,29)
B34:  2
C34:  (,2)  62.64
D34:  (,2)  +B34*C34
E34:  (,2)  +$F$11*B34
F34:  (P2)  (+$F$12*4)/C34
G34:  (,2)  +B34*(AA34+$F$11)-D34
H34:  (P2)  +G34/D34
A35:  (D1)  @DATE(83,5,15)
B35:  2
C35:  (,2)  62.27
D35:  (,2)  +B35*C35
E35:  (,2)  +$F$11*B35
F35:  (P2)  (+$F$12*4)/C35
G35:  (,2)  +B35*(AA35+$F$11)-D35
H35:  (P2)  +G35/D35
A36:  (D1)  @DATE(83,8,31)
B36:  1
C36:  (,2)  60.52
D36:  (,2)  +B36*C36
E36:  (,2)  +$F$11*B36
F36:  (P2)  (+$F$12*4)/C36
G36:  (,2)  +B36*(AA36+$F$11)-D36
H36:  (P2)  +G36/D36
A37:  (D1)  @DATE(83,9,15)

B37:  2
C37:  (,2)  63.97
D37:  (,2)  +B37*C37
E37:  (,2)  +$F$11*B37
F37:  (P2)  (+$F$12*4)/C37
G37:  (,2)  +B37*(AA37+$F$11)-D37
H37:  (P2)  +G37/D37
A38:  (D1)  @DATE(83,9,27)
B38:  2
C38:  (,2)  72
D38:  (,2)  +B38*C38
E38:  (,2)  +$F$11*B38
F38:  (P2)  (+$F$12*4)/C38
G38:  (,2)  +B38*(AA38+$F$11)-D38
H38:  (P2)  +G38/D38
A39:  (D1)  @DATE(83,9,30)
B39:  2
C39:  (,2)  78.22
D39:  (,2)  +B39*C39
E39:  (,2)  +$F$11*B39
F39:  (P2)  (+$F$12*4)/C39
G39:  (,2)  +B39*(AA39+$F$11)-D39
H39:  (P2)  +G39/D39
A40:  (D1)  @DATE(83,10,14)
B40:  1
C40:  (,2)  72.42
D40:  (,2)  +B40*C40
E40:  (,2)  +$F$11*B40
F40:  (P2)  (+$F$12*4)/C40
G40:  (,2)  +B40*(AA40+$F$11)-D40
H40:  (P2)  +G40/D40
A41:  (D1)  @DATE(83,10,31)
B41:  2
C41:  (,2)  78.7
D41:  (,2)  +B41*C41
E41:  (,2)  +$F$11*B41
F41:  (P2)  (+$F$12*4)/C41
G41:  (,2)  +B41*(AA41+$F$11)-D41
H41:  (P2)  +G41/D41
A42:  (D1)  @DATE(83,11,15)
B42:  2
C42:  (,2)  76.95
D42:  (,2)  +B42*C42
E42:  (,2)  +$F$11*B42
F42:  (P2)  (+$F$12*4)/C42
G42:  (,2)  +B42*(AA42+$F$11)-D42
H42:  (P2)  +G42/D42
A43:  (D1)  @DATE(83,11,30)
B43:  2
C43:  (,2)  81.9
D43:  (,2)  +B43*C43
E43:  (,2)  +$F$11*B43
F43:  (P2)  (+$F$12*4)/C43
G43:  (,2)  +B43*(AA43+$F$11)-D43
```

```
H43:  (P2)  +G43/D43                    F46:  (C2)  \=
A44:  (D1)  @DATE(83,12,15)             G46:  (,2)  \=
B44:  1                                 H46:  (C2)  \=
C44:  (,2)  72.48                       B47:  @SUM(B45..B18)
D44:  (,2)  +B44*C44                    C47:  (C2)  @AVG(C44..C18)
E44:  (,2)  +$F$11*B44                  D47:  (C2)  @SUM(D44..D18)
F44:  (P2)  (+$F$12*4)/C44              E47:  (C2)  @SUM(E44..E18)
G44:  (,2)  +B44*(AA44+$F$11)-D44       F47:  (P2)  @AVG(F44..F18)
H44:  (P2)  +G44/D44                    G47:  (C2)  @SUM(G44..G18)
A45:  (D1)  @DATE(83,12,30)             H47:  (P2)  +G47/D47
B45:  2                                 A49:  '        MINIMUM =
C45:  (,2)  74.29                       C49:  (C2)  @MIN(C45..C18)
D45:  (,2)  +B45*C45                    E49:  '          MAXIMUM =
E45:  (,2)  +$F$11*B45                  G49:  (C2)  @MAX(C18..C45)
F45:  (P2)  (+$F$12*4)/C45              A51:  'JAMES T. SOMEBODY CAN BORROW
G45:  (,2)  +B45*(AA45+$F$11)-D45       ON SMC STOCK PLAN
H45:  (P2)  +G45/D45                    A52:  (P2)  0.75
A46:  (D1)  \=                          B52:  ' OF  TODAY'S TOTAL VALUE
B46:  (D1)  \=                          E52:  (C2)  +E47
C46:  (,2)  \=                          F52:  (P2)  'i.e.,
D46:  (,2)  \=                          G52:  (C2)  +E52*A52
E46:  (,2)  \=                          G53:  (C2)  \=
```

Bibliography

Bailard, Thomas E. Biehl, David L.; and Kaiser, Ronald W. *Personal Money Management*. Chicago; SRA, 1977.

Dorfman, John. *Family Investment Guide*. NY; Atheneum, 1982.

Gourgues, Harold W. Jr. *Financial Planning Handbook*. NY; NY Institute of Finance, 1983.

Hallman, G. Victor and Rosenbloom, Jerry S. *Personal Financial Planning*. NY; McGraw-Hill, 1981.

Hardy, C. Colburn. *Your Money & Your Life*. NY; Amacom, 1982.

Randle, Paul A. and Swensen, Philip R. *Personal Financial Planning for Executives*. CA; Lifetime Learning Publications, 1982.

——————. *Managing Your Money*. CA; Lifetime Learning Publications, 1979.

Richardson, Gayle E. *Am I Covered?* Indiana; Unified College Press, Inc. 1973.

Rosefsky, Bob. *Money Talks*. NY; John Wiley & Sons, Inc. 1982.

Smith, Milton. *Money Today More Tomorrow*. MA; Winthrop Publishers, 1981.

Stillman, Richard J. *Your Personal Financial Planner*. NJ; Prentice-Hall, 1981.

Van Caspel, Venita. *The Power of Money Dynamics*. Virginia; Reston Publishing Co. 1983.

Index

About the Author

Nick Maffei literally grew up with computers. In 1955 he graduated first in his class from the U.S. Army Data processing School in Fort Devens, Massachusetts, and went on assignment in Europe with the Army Security Agency. From there he worked his way through college and graduate school as a computer programmer.

Today Nick Maffei is a Small Systems Specialist with IBM Corporation in San Francisco. His IBM background includes 20 years experience as a systems engineer, marketing representative, teacher, lecturer and writer.

Mr. Maffei has taught at several schools and colleges in Florida and California and has written a variety of articles for *PC Magazine* and other computer publications. In addition, he is a licensed real estate agent and operates his own property management firm.

His educational background includes a B.S. degree from Florida State University and an M.B.A. degree in Finance from Golden Gate University in San Francisco.

OTHER POPULAR TAB BOOKS OF INTEREST

| TAB | TAB BOOKS Inc.

Blue Ridge Summit, Pa. 17214

Send for FREE TAB Catalog describing over 750 current titles in print.

Money Management
Worksheets for 1-2-3™/Symphony™

If you are intrigued with the possibilities of the spreadsheets included in *Money Management Worksheets for 1-2-3/Symphony* (TAB BOOK No. 1968), you should definitely consider having the ready-to-run disk containing the software applications. This software is guaranteed free of manufacturer's defects. (If you have any problems, return the disk within 30 days, and we'll send you a new one.) Not only will you save the time and effort of typing the spreadsheets, the disk eliminates the possibility of errors that can prevent the spreadsheets from functioning. Interested?

Available on disk for IBM PC with Lotus 1-2-3, 256K.

Available on disk for IBM PC with Symphony, 320K at $19.95 for each disk plus $1.00 each shipping and handling.